MW00988509

TURNING POINTS

RUSSELL SHAW

TURNING POINTS

How Thirteen Remarkable
Men and Women
Heard God's Call
and Responded to It

IGNATIUS PRESS   SAN FRANCISCO

Cover images (from top, clockwise):

SAINT THÉRÈSE OF LISIEUX: At 15 years old. 1885. Photographer unknown

SAINT AUGUSTINE OF HIPPO: *Painting of Augustine of Hippo and his mother Monica of Hippo*:
Ary Scheffer (1795–1858): National Gallery, London

SAINT JOSEMARÍA ESCRIVÁ: Founder of Opus Dei. 23 September 1966.
Oficina de Información de la Prelatura del Opus Dei en España

SAINT BENEDICT JOSEPH LABRE: Colour lithograph. Wellcome Library, London

DOROTHY DAY: American journalist, social activist, and Catholic convert.
Photographer unknown

SAINT TERESA OF AVILA: Painting by Eduardo Balaca (1840–1914), Museo del Prado,
Madrid, Spain

SAINT IGNATIUS LOYOLA: Line engraving by J. Caron, 1842. Wellcome Library, London

C. S. LEWIS: As an undergraduate at University College, Trinity Term in 1917.
[Wikimedia Commons]

POPE SAINT PAUL VI: Photo from University of Urbino (circa 1963).
Photographer unknown

CARYLL HOUSELANDER: Photographer unknown

SAINT PAUL THE APOSTLE: *Medallion with Saint Paul from an Icon Frame*:
Metropolitan Museum of Art. Gift of J. Pierpont Morgan, 1917

SAINT JOHN HENRY NEWMAN: Photographic portrait by Herbert Rose Barraud.
(Unknown date, probably between circa 1885 and circa 1890.) [Wikimedia Commons]

SAINT THOMAS MORE: Portrait by Hans Holbein the Younger,
Frick Collection, New York. [Wikimedia Commons]

Cover design by Pawel Cetlinski

© 2025 by Ignatius Press, San Francisco
All rights reserved
ISBN 978-1-62164-772-0 (PB)
ISBN 978-1-64229-348-7 (eBook)
Library of Congress Control Number 2024950097
Printed in the United States of America ⊗

For Carmen

CONTENTS

INTRODUCTION

Some years ago, Jean Kerr, a witty chronicler of the tragi-comedies of family life, drew the title of one of her books from something one of her youngsters said. Coming home from school one day, the little boy reported that the first grade was rehearsing a playlet on the fall of Adam and Eve. Then he added bitterly, "The snake has all the lines."

Sometimes, when evildoers hog the attention, it really can seem that way. But evildoing tends to be repetitious—the Bible lumps sinning under only ten general headings—while there is a splendid variety in the ways of being good. This book tells the stories of thirteen people who were notable for doing that.

It is not simply a collection of saints' lives, though. It is that, of course, but it is also something more—an attempt to identify the turning points in those lives, the special incidents or episodes that led each person to see and embrace the unique role intended for him or her in God's providential plan.

What does a life-changing turning point look like? As the stories illustrate, it can take many forms and is adapted to the special circumstances of the individual receiving it. In a sermon titled "Divine Calls", Saint John Henry Newman provides an example that has the merit of being something we can all imagine happening to us.

"A man is going on as usual", he writes. "He comes home one day, and finds a letter or a message or a person whereby a sudden trial comes on him which, if met

9

religiously, will be the means of advancing him to a higher state of religious excellence, which at present he as little comprehends as the unspeakable words heard by St. Paul in paradise." The form such a communication takes is a matter of indifference, Newman remarks, provided "we feel it to be a command".[1]

The turning points examined here range from the highly dramatic (e.g., Saint Paul's experience on the road to Damascus, which was precisely what was required to make a lasting impact on Paul) to the intensely personalized (Dorothy Day's first encounter with French peasant-philosopher Peter Maurin at the very time she was yearning to play a role in creating a just social order). For Newman, the turning point—the decision to seek admission to the Catholic Church—came, as you would expect of a man of scholarly, bookish habits, following months of intense study, writing, and prayer.

Each biographical sketch is followed by a brief section offering general observations arising from the biography.

Along with describing turning points, the book represents further consideration of a subject I have written about before—personal vocation. Every Christian receives a call to one of these, and each call is uniquely his own; and turning points generally occur in the context of personal vocations, although, if God so chooses, the turning point in someone's life may *be* the discernment of his personal vocation.

Pope Saint John Paul II speaks of these matters clearly and forcefully in *Christifideles Laici*, his apostolic exhortation on the laity and their role in the Church and in the world. Declaring the "fundamental objective" of lay

---

[1] John Henry Newman, "Divine Calls", in *Parochial and Plain Sermons* (San Francisco: Ignatius Press, 1987), 1570.

formation to be "an ever-clearer discovery of one's vocation and the ever-greater willingness to live it so as to fulfill
one's mission", John Paul says that "from eternity God has
thought of us and has loved us as unique individuals." But
the specifics of one's personal vocation are disclosed in "a
gradual process ... one that happens day by day". Adoles-
cence and young adulthood are particularly sensitive periods for vocational discernment, yet the Lord calls "at every
hour of life so as to make his holy will more precisely and
explicitly known", thus requiring steady "vigilance and a
conscious attentiveness to the voice of God".[2]

I hope this book will help many readers in their continuing efforts to be attentive to God's call in the events of
their lives. The rewards are very great, as Romano Guardini points out: "If a man is conscious of the fact that God
has created him by calling him forth, so that he is one who
is addressed by God; if he regards the various situations
of his life as modes of this call, and his own action as the
answers he gives, then the core of his person becomes more
and more solid, secure and free; his nature becomes ever
richer and more receptive of eternity." Whereas, Guardini stresses, the consequences of the most extreme form
of rejecting this option—atheism—can be dire: for in that
case a human person "no longer knows who he is".[3]

I hope, too, that this book will make it emphatically
clear that in the final analysis, the snake does *not* have all
the lines.

---

[2] John Paul II, apostolic exhortation *Christifideles Laici* (December 30, 1988),
no. 58.
[3] Romano Guardini, *The Wisdom of the Psalms*, in *The World and the Person:
And Other Writings*, trans. Stella Lange (Washington, D.C.: Regnery, 2023),
528–29.

Saint Paul the Apostle

(ca. A.D. 5–65)

The Persecutor Who Became an Apostle

Before the event that would forever change his life, Saul of Tarsus was certain with the certainty of a fanatic that he knew what God wanted him to do about the problem that obsessed him.

Not so long before, this Pharisee of Pharisees had stood by and watched with satisfaction while the Christian deacon Stephen was stoned to death (see Acts 7:58—8:1). Now, picking up where the assassins had left off, Saul was on his way to Damascus with a commission from the high priest himself to seize any Christians he found there and bring them, bound, back to Jerusalem. For it was clear to him beyond the shadow of a doubt that this detestable sect, with its claim to have a messianic leader who had risen from the dead, posed a mortal threat to his beloved Judaism and had to be destroyed.

Then it happened: something unforeseen and so utterly remarkable that it is recorded in detail no fewer than three times in the Acts of the Apostles. Here is how Paul—the new name he would soon adopt in recognition of the radical change he had experienced—described it:

> As I made my journey and drew near to Damascus, about noon a great light from heaven suddenly shone about me.

And I fell to the ground and heard a voice saying to me,
"Saul, Saul, why do you persecute me?" And I answered,
"Who are you, Lord?" And he said to me, "I am Jesus
of Nazareth whom you are persecuting." ... And I said,
"What shall I do, Lord?" And the Lord said to me, "Rise,
and go into Damascus, and there you will be told all that
is appointed for you to do." And when I could not see
because of the brightness of that light, I was led by the
hand by those who were with me. (22:6–11)

When he reached Damascus, Paul was at first under-
standably regarded with some apprehension by Jesus' followers there, but they eventually accepted him as an
authentic convert to the faith. From that point on, much of
the remainder of the Acts of the Apostles tells the story
of Paul and his wide-ranging and adventure-filled ministry
as the Apostle to the Gentiles. It is a sometimes harrowing account of a man's heroism and perseverance—and
frequent displays of extraordinary chutzpah—in preaching
the Christian message to the surrounding pagan society
after failing to crack the indifference of his fellow Jews,
which often turned into violent hostility. It is a story that
makes it abundantly clear why Pope Saint John Paul II
honored Paul as Jesus' "herald".

But until that turning point on the road to Damascus,
there was nothing in Paul's background or career to suggest anything of the sort. Quite the contrary.

He was born around A.D. 5 in Tarsus, a busy trading city
on the southeastern coast of modern-day Turkey. His parents were devout Jews and adherents of the Pharisee sect.
As we know from the Gospels, many Pharisees in Jesus'
day had become wedded to a legalistic religiosity that
stressed the external minutiae of religion, looked down on
others, and nurtured a spirit of blind intolerance that made
them deadly enemies of Jesus.

Yet some, retaining the original ideals of the Pharisees, were high-minded reformers committed to upholding and defending the faithful observance of the Law of Moses. The Gospel of Luke reports that concerned Pharisees went to Jesus to warn him that the local ruler, Herod Antipas, was seeking his life (see 13:31). Acts tells us that Paul studied the Law under the eminent teacher Gamaliel, a Pharisee (see 22:3), and that this same Gamaliel cautioned the Jewish Sanhedrin, which had seized the apostles Peter and John, to be careful in its treatment of them since the message they preached could be of God (see 5:38–39).

As a youth growing up in Tarsus, Paul learned the trade of tent making; then, as a young man, he traveled to Jerusalem for religious studies. "I advanced in Judaism beyond many of my own age among my people, so extremely zealous was I for the traditions of my fathers", he later wrote (Gal 1:14). Christianity was in its early days, but hostility toward it was already on the rise. On one notable occasion, Saul watched approvingly as local Jews, infuriated at the outspoken proclamation of the new faith by the Christian deacon Stephen, stoned him to death. Inflamed by their example, Saul turned to being an active persecutor himself, as Acts reports: "Entering house after house, he dragged off men and women and committed them to prison" (8:3).

After obtaining a commission from the Jewish high priest, he set out for Damascus intending to continue there his one-man crusade against Jesus' followers. And then came that dramatic encounter on the road and those accusing words, "Saul, Saul, why do you persecute me?" Saul, the aspiring archpersecutor of Christians, was transformed in a literally blinding flash into Paul, one singled out by Jesus Christ himself to be his herald and preacher.

But why did God reach out in this way to a zealous enemy of Christ? As always, God had his reasons, not all of them necessarily known to us. But this much is clear:

it had always been true that Saul could—and very likely did—say with the psalmist, "Zeal for your house has consumed me" (Ps 69:9). Horribly wrongheaded though Saul the persecutor had been in hating Christians and seeking to crush Christianity, now that the Lord himself had made him know better, his energy, intelligence, and zeal made him particularly useful in the cause of spreading the new faith. This was particularly the case in light of Paul's readiness to preach the gospel to the Gentiles, whom Jewish converts, the larger part of the early Christian community, often hesitated to receive unless the Gentiles observed the Jewish Law as they themselves continued to do.

Between roughly A.D. 45 and 58, Saint Paul made three principal missionary journeys during which he traveled through much of Asia Minor and eventually Macedonia and Greece. Typically, on arriving in a new town, he began by speaking in the local synagogue; if his message was rejected there, as commonly happened, he would preach the good news of redemption in Christ to the Gentiles. Sometimes he and his message were received joyfully; other times, he was violently dismissed, even at threat to his life.

Paul is unsurpassed as a chronicler of his agonies and ecstasies in the service of Jesus, as in this vivid passage in his second letter to his converts in the Greek city of Corinth:

Five times I have received at the hands of the Jews the forty lashes less one. Three times I have been beaten with rods; once I was stoned. Three times I have been shipwrecked; a night and a day I have been adrift at sea; on frequent journeys, in danger from rivers, danger from robbers, danger from my own people, danger from Gentiles, danger in the city, danger in the wilderness, danger at sea, danger from false brethren; in toil and hardship, through many a sleepless night, in hunger and thirst, often without food, in cold and exposure. (2 Cor 11:24–27)

Then, shifting gears, he speaks of "a man"—himself, of course—who years before had been "caught up into Paradise" and there granted extraordinary revelations. After this, he hastens to note that he suffers from an unspecified, chronic affliction—"a thorn ... in the flesh, a messenger of Satan"— that serves the Lord's purpose by keeping him humble. "For the sake of Christ, then", Paul concludes, "I am content with weaknesses, insults, hardships, persecutions, and calamities; for when I am weak, then I am strong" (2 Cor 12:1–10). As this suggests, Paul was not one to keep his feelings to himself; his emotions were close to the surface and readily expressed. Reading him can be an emotional roller-coaster ride, full of dazzling ascents and dizzying drops. Quick to declare his resentment of others' criticism and rejection for his identifying with Jesus, he took these as criticism and rejection of his Lord as well. After all, as he unabashedly explained, "I have been crucified with Christ; it is no longer I who live, but Christ who lives in me" (Gal 2:20).

Along with being a dynamic evangelizer, Paul was an important source of Christian doctrine. The letters that he addressed to his new Christian converts with the aim of strengthening them in the faith contain passage after passage of teaching fundamental to the faith we profess today as members of the Church. That includes such crucial matters as the nature and mission of Jesus Christ—the redemptive significance of his life and death, his bodily Resurrection, the effects of baptism in Christ, his Real Presence in the Eucharist, the Church as his Mystical Body, the offices and charisms found in the Church, and the justifying power of faith in him—as well as numerous moral norms and a brief exposition of natural law as the law "written on ... hearts" (Rom 2:15).

Besides particular doctrines, Paul's contribution is of great importance in affirming the radical difference between

Christianity's grounding in matters of fact and paganism's grounding in myth. As a young theologian, Joseph Ratzinger—the future Pope Benedict XVI—made this point in his well-known *Introduction to Christianity*, citing the first chapter of the Letter to the Romans in which Paul accounts for "the fate of the ancient religion by the division between *logos* [word] and myth: 'For what can be known about God is plain to them [i.e., the pagans], because God has shown it to them ... [but] although they knew God they did not honor him as God or give thanks to him.... [They] exchanged the glory of the immortal God for images resembling mortal man or birds or animals or reptiles' (Rom 1:19–23)." By contrast, Ratzinger continues, and thanks in no small part to Paul, Christianity "put itself resolutely on the side of truth and thus turned its back on a conception of religion satisfied to be mere outward ceremonial which in the end can be interpreted to mean anything one fancies".[1]

Beyond the immediate challenge of paganism, Paul also led the way in combating Gnosticism, the heresy that was to bedevil Christianity for centuries. Starting from the premise of radical opposition between spirit and matter, the Gnostics held, in Guardini's words, that Christ, the Logos, "had only a phantom body on earth, lived a phantom life and died only in appearance".[2] In doing so, of course, they undermined the reality of the Incarnation at its roots.

Paul's reply to this could hardly be clearer: "Have this mind among yourselves, which was in Christ Jesus, who, though he was in the form of God, did not count equality with God a thing to be grasped, but emptied himself,

[1] Joseph Ratzinger, *Introduction to Christianity* (New York: Crossroad, 1988), 96–97.

[2] Romano Guardini, *The Church of the Lord*, in *The World and the Person: And Other Writings*, trans. Stella Lange (Washington, D.C.: Regnery, 2023), 465.

taking the form of a servant, being born in the likeness of men. And being found in human form he humbled himself and became obedient unto death" (Phil 2:5–8). And this: "When the time had fully come, God sent forth his Son, born of woman, born under the law ... so that we might receive adoption as sons" (Gal 4:4–5).

Of central importance in Paul's career was his prolonged and sometimes acrimonious argument with the Judaizers—those Jewish converts to Christianity who held that Gentile converts should receive circumcision and observe Jewish dietary laws. Paul strenuously rejected that viewpoint, not just because it placed an undue burden on Gentile converts but also and especially because it implicitly denied the life-changing and definitive newness of faith in Christ.

In his letter to his Christian converts in Philippi, he offered an autobiographical response to the Judaizers, declaring himself to be as good a Jew as any of them— "circumcised on the eighth day, of the people of Israel, of the tribe of Benjamin, a Hebrew born of Hebrews; as to the law a Pharisee, as to zeal a persecutor of the Church, as to righteousness under the law blameless." And then he added his conclusive bottom line: "But whatever gain I had, I counted as loss for the sake of Christ" (Phil 3:5–7).

Eventually the quarrel was settled by a gathering described in chapter 15 of the Acts of the Apostles and now commonly referred to as the Council of Jerusalem. After Saint Peter spoke tellingly in support of Paul's position, Paul proceeded to make his case. The assembled Christian elders then decided in favor of Paul, imposing only a few minor requirements on the Gentile converts.

Not only was Paul vindicated, but also the Church was set firmly on the path of evangelization that she still follows. And after the Jerusalem council, Paul, writing to

Christians in the region of Galatia, explained the foundation of his own faith with his customary vigor: "I have been crucified with Christ; it is no longer I who live, but Christ who lives in me; and the life I now live in the flesh I live by faith in the Son of God, who loved me and gave himself for me" (Gal 2:20).

Around A.D. 65, in Rome by now, Saint Paul was executed by beheading during the persecution of Christians ordered by the emperor Nero. But his indomitable spirit and soaring words live on. That dramatic turning point on the road to Damascus had deep and lasting consequences—not only for Paul of Tarsus but, ever since, for Jesus' Church.

While situating Paul in his account of the profound relationship between vocation and the providence of God, Romano Guardini paints a striking picture of him as he was before his encounter with Jesus on the road to Damascus: "a passionate, strongwilled character with a deep longing for salvation, but interiorly restrained in many ways. In the long discipline of Pharisaic piety this man had become a stern zealot for the ancestral law but had thereby fallen into the deepest distress. Convinced that he must attain his salvation by the fulfilling of the law, he had discovered that he was incapable of doing this. The violence which he imposed upon himself only submerged the evil and did not remove it"—a tension that he attempted to relieve by the external violence of persecuting the new Church. It was in this divided and troubled state of mind that he found himself confronted and challenged by Christ and that he underwent deep and lasting change.[3]

---

[3] Romano Guardini, *The World and the Person* in *The World and the Person*, 359.

Here we find what Guardini calls the "root" of vocation as it was present in Saul of Tarsus prior to his conversion. After that event, it interacted with divine providence to produce the results visible in the Paul of Acts and the letters, as well as in the Christian communities that he evangelized on his missionary journeys.

Divine providence is, of course, active in the world where and when and how God wills, but there is one place, Guardini says, where it enters "surely and regularly, as soon as the required conditions are present: namely, the existence of the person who believes and who loves the kingdom of God.... This is the constant miracle, whose proclamation was the most intimate concern of Jesus, the miracle of Christian existence, the development of the new world around the child of God", and it is most clearly visible in "those who heroically and unconditionally risked everything for it, the saints".[4] This, to a preeminent degree, was the history of the post-Damascus Paul.

Ultimately, Guardini concludes, the fulfillment brought about by providence will be eschatological—"it looks toward what is to come"—and here he quotes a famous passage in Paul's Letter to the Romans: "I consider that the sufferings of this present time are not worth comparing with the glory that is to be revealed to us. For the creation waits with eager longing for the revealing of the sons of God; for the creation was subjected to futility, not of its own will but by the will of him who subjected it in hope; because the creation itself will be set free from its bondage to decay and obtain the glorious liberty of the children of God" (8:18–21).

Paul's experience was uniquely his own, as is true of any individual's immediate experience of God's presence and action in his life. Yet the general pattern can be seen

[4] Ibid., 396–97.

at work elsewhere—sometimes in surprising ways. Flannery O'Connor titled her second novel *The Violent Bear It Away*—that being her own translation of a saying of Christ in the eleventh chapter of Matthew's Gospel: "From the days of John the Baptist until now, the kingdom of heaven suffereth violence, and the violent bear it away" (see v. 12). And when a correspondent asked her why she, a Catholic, wrote about fundamentalist Protestants rather than Catholics, this was her answer:

> About the fanatics. People make a judgment of fanaticism by what they are themselves. To a lot of Protestants I know, monks and nuns are fanatics, none greater. And to a lot of the monks and nuns I know, my Protestant prophets are fanatics. For my part, I think the only difference between them is that if you are a Catholic and have this intensity of belief you join the convent and are heard from no more; whereas if you are a Protestant and have it, there is no convent for you to join and you go about in the world, getting into all sorts of trouble and drawing the wrath of people who don't believe anything at all down on your head.

To this she added that a fundamentalist preacher in one of her stories was actually a "crypto-Catholic", explaining, "When you leave a man alone with his Bible and the Holy Ghost inspires him, he's going to be a Catholic one way or another, even though he knows nothing about the visible church."[5]

Times have changed since O'Connor said that. For one thing, by comparison with the 1950s, when seminaries and convents were filled to capacity, far fewer people in

---

[5] Letter to Sister Mariella Gable, May 1963, in *Flannery O'Connor: Collected Works* (New York: Library of America, 1988), 1183.

America enter the religious life or the priesthood today, so that the work of preserving and spreading the faith now rests with the laity perhaps more than ever. Considered in that light, the great temptation of our times may lie in professing and practicing a kind of Christianity that is merely "nice"—a bland, give-no-offense, don't-rock-the-boat version of the faith, of which the best thing to be said may be that it is not going to upset anyone.

Strong doses of Saint Paul could be an antidote to that— the Paul who, hauled before a petty king named Agrippa and ordered to give an account of himself, met Agrippa's sneering comment "In a short time you think to make me a Christian!" with the bold response "Whether short or long, I would to God that not only you but all who hear me this day might become such as I am—except for these chains" (Acts 26:28–29). Spoken like a real prophet, you might say.

Saint Augustine of Hippo

(A.D. 354–August 28, 430)

The Saint of the Restless Heart

"Our hearts are restless until they rest in you." Addressed to God, these famous words of Saint Augustine come at the start of his account of how a headstrong, self-indulgent, yet unquestionably brilliant young man became one of the most important Christian thinkers of all time—and a saint. Saint Augustine tells the story of his conversion in his *Confessions*, a volume that is itself a landmark in spiritual and literary history and has fascinated readers for centuries.

Do not look here for a flattering self-portrait of the author, though. As one of the book's many translators explains, *Confessions* was written largely to "persuade [Augustine's] admirers that any good qualities he had were his by the grace of God, who had saved him so often from himself".[1] In this, clearly, the volume succeeds, perhaps even beyond Augustine's hopes.

He was born in the year 354 in Thagaste (also spelled Tagaste), a Roman town in what is now Algeria. His father, Patricius, was a Roman landowner and a minor official; his mother, Monica, a devout Christian who ultimately won her husband over to Christianity. Recognizing their son's

---

[1] R. S. Pine-Coffin, introduction to *Confessions*, by Saint Augustine, trans. R. S. Pine-Coffin (New York: Penguin Classics, 1961), 12.

intellectual giftedness, his parents, though by no means wealthy, sent him as a youth to study in Carthage—a city Augustine later described as "a hissing cauldron of lust"— where, finding it all too easy to indulge his passions, he took a mistress and fathered a son, whom he called Adeodatus, "Given by God".

But along with all this, he nevertheless was at the head of his class in rhetoric—an important discipline in those days, when the skill of speaking well in public was an essential tool in practicing law, holding public office, and other occupations. At the age of nineteen, however, he read a book by the Roman statesman and philosopher Cicero that moved him to adopt the pursuit of truth as the guiding rationale of his studies. And now began the tug and pull of conflicting interests that were to plague him for years. "Give me chastity and continence, but not yet", he prayed.[2]

Monica had been careful to see that he became a catechumen while still a child, but, as was common at that time, his baptism had been delayed. Now, reading the Bible and finding that it failed to measure up to his sophisticated literary tastes, the clever young man turned instead to the Manichaeans, a popular sect notable for "dazzling fantasies" about the origins of evil.

Horrified, his pious mother begged a Christian bishop to tell her son to break off this attachment. "Leave him alone", the bishop told her. "He will see their errors for himself." The bishop was right. When Carthage was visited by a Manichaean leader named Faustus, who enjoyed a reputation for wisdom, Augustine peppered him with questions and found him to be intellectually shallow. Yet,

---

[2] Saint Augustine, *Confessions*, trans. R. S. Pine-Coffin (New York: Penguin Classics, 1961), 169.

still thinking he had nothing better to turn to, Augustine remained loosely associated with the Manichaeans.

Having taught rhetoric for a time in Thagaste and Carthage and grown increasingly disgusted with the rowdy behavior of his students, the young professor moved to Rome in 383, intending to teach there. The following year, he was offered an attractive teaching position in Milan, at that time the seat of the imperial government, and moved there. He also made the acquaintance of the local Catholic bishop, Ambrose, and began attending church to hear him preach—not for the message of the homilies, of course, but for the excellence of Bishop Ambrose's literary style. After a while, nevertheless, the substance of what this future saint was saying started to sink in—so much so, in fact, that Augustine now made a final break with the Manichaeans. Yet, despite feeling increasingly drawn to Christianity, he hesitated to become a Christian for fear of being wrong again.

And, then too, there were certain other ties that he did not care to break.

Upon turning thirty, he put a question to himself: "Why do I delay? Why do I not abandon my worldly hopes and give myself up entirely to the search for God and the life of true happiness?" But of course he already knew the answer: "Not so fast! This life is too sweet. It has its own charms." Worldly esteem, marriage to a woman of wealth, and a bit of respectable sensuality on the side—with an enjoyable life like that in hand, he told himself, he might even find a little time to spare for intellectual pursuits.

As a result of Monica's efforts, he made a commitment to marry a young woman of good family, but the girl was underage, and their marriage was therefore postponed for two years. Now he broke with his mistress, and she returned to Africa. But his "disease of the flesh" persisted, and he took a new mistress in place of the old, even as he wrestled with theological questions about the nature of God. Augustine, in short, was suffering from a mental error not uncommon in people who pride themselves on their high intelligence: trusting their superior brains to solve their problems and settle their doubts instead of turning trustingly to God and placing themselves unconditionally in his hands.

Now, though, he took what would prove to be a fateful step—he began reading and reflecting on the letters of Saint Paul. The words of that fiery convert who called himself "the least of the apostles" (1 Cor 15:9) made a deep impression, and Paul's praise of continence as a way of life especially struck home. But, even so, Augustine continued to be a man torn by "two wills ... one the servant of the flesh, the other of the spirit".[3]

August of the year 386 found him staying at a wealthy friend's country villa with Monica and his close friend Alypius. One day, tormented as usual by his questions and doubts, Augustine went into the garden and, weeping bitterly, flung himself down under a fig tree. Suddenly he heard what he supposed to be the voice of a child singing the same refrain over and over: "Take it and read, take it and read."

Augustine recalls what happened next:

> I looked up, thinking hard whether there was any kind of game in which children used to chant words like these, but I could not remember ever hearing them before. I stemmed my flood of tears and stood up, telling myself that this could only be a divine command to open my book of Scripture and read the first passage....
>
> I had put down the book containing Paul's Epistles....
> In silence I read the first passage [in chapter 13 of the Letter to the Romans] on which my eyes fell: *Not in revelling and drunkenness, not in lust and wantonness, not in quarrels*

[3] Ibid., 164.

and rivalries. Rather, arm yourselves with the Lord Jesus Christ;
spend no more thought on nature and nature's appetites. I had
no wish to read more.... It was as though the light of
confidence flooded into my heart and all the darkness of
doubt was dispelled.[4]

Upon going into the house, he told Monica what had
happened. "She was jubilant with triumph", he writes, still
addressing God. "For she saw that you had granted her far
more than she used to ask in her tearful prayers and plain-
tive lamentations. You converted me to yourself."[5]

Augustine, Alypius, and Adeodatus were baptized on
Holy Saturday the following year. Monica, her dreams ful-
filled, died that autumn. Augustine returned to Thagaste,
and Adeodatus, who had accompanied him, died not long
after. Augustine was living a kind of lay monasticism when
the bishop of Hippo, a coastal town not far from Carthage,
persuaded him to be ordained. In 396 he became the bishop's assistant. The following year, Augustine succeeded
him as bishop of Hippo.

Now, along with pastoral duties, Augustine wrote pro-
lifically, composing a stream of theological and scriptural
studies, as well as thousands of letters and homilies. Near
the end of his life, responding to a Roman official who
had sent him a letter filled with compliments, he enclosed
a copy of the *Confessions* and added this: "In these behold
me, that you may not praise me beyond what I am; in these
believe what is said of me, not by others but by myself....
Indeed, we had destroyed ourselves, but He who made us
has made us anew."[6]

---

[4] Ibid., 177–78.
[5] Ibid., 178.
[6] Quoted in Peter Brown, *Augustine of Hippo* (Berkeley: University of Cali-
fornia Press, 1969), 427.

In 429, the Vandals, a warlike Germanic people who adhered to the Arian heresy and are best known for sacking Rome in 455, as the Goths had done forty-five years earlier, crossed over from Spain to North Africa and began moving east along the Mediterranean coast. In short order, they reached and besieged Hippo. As the Roman world he had known crumbled around him, on August 28, 430, Augustine died quietly.

Saint Augustine's two greatest literary achievements are the *Confessions* and the massive *City of God*, which was to serve as a basic text during the Middle Ages and continues to be read with appreciation. His influence on later Christian thinking is apparent to anyone skimming the writing of Saint Thomas Aquinas and observing the sheer quantity of references to Augustine in the works of the thirteenth-century master. The historian of philosophy Frederick Copleston, S.J., states a simple fact in saying that Aquinas "naturally treads in the footsteps of Augustine".[7] But the *Confessions* occupies a unique place as the first true autobiography and one of the finest—a gripping account of the struggle of a man of genius with his own intellectual pride and deep-seated weakness of the flesh before the turning point at which he placed himself unreservedly in the service of God.

While the conversion of Saint Augustine was a definitive turning away from his addiction to sins of unchastity, that experience of turning away from something was intrinsically linked to a final and definitive act of turning *to* some

---

[7] Frederick Copleston, "Aquinas and Augustine", in *St. Thomas Aquinas on Politics and Ethics*, ed. Paul E. Sigmund (New York: Norton, 1988), 134.

one, for in this life-changing act, Augustine totally and once and for all committed himself to faith in Jesus Christ. Indeed, the two things were not separate and distinct acts of intellect and will but a single, comprehensive turning to the Lord: "You saw how deep I was sunk in death, and it was your power that drained dry the well of corruption in the depths of my heart. And all that you asked of me was to deny my own will and accept yours."[8]

The weakness of the flesh that was so much a part of the young Augustine was not unique to him then, nor is it uncommon today—a time when the internet is flooded with pornography and out-of-wedlock births make up 40 percent of the U.S. total.[9] The contemporary world has been described as a "moral pigsty",[10] and the only exception one might reasonably take to that characterization is that it is unfair to pigs. Critics sometimes accuse Augustine of being overly concerned with sexual morality (and the same charge is often lodged against the Catholic Church), but it is an odd critique indeed at a time when sexual obsession and sexual immorality are blatantly obvious facts of modern secular life. Sins against chastity are, to be sure, not the only kinds of sin, and sins of cruelty, violence, and injustice abound in today's world. At the same time, however, it appears that sins of unchastity do lie at or close to the fetid heart of contemporary evildoing.

Be that as it may, Augustine himself is a great deal more balanced on the subject of sex than his critics care to admit.

---

[8] Augustine, *Confessions*, 181.

[9] Michelle J. K. Osterman et al., "Births: Final Data for 2022", *National Vital Statistics Reports* 73, no. 2 (April 4, 2024): 5, https://www.cdc.gov/nchs/data/nvsr/nvsr73/nvsr73-02.pdf.

[10] Archbishop Anthony Fisher, O.P., "The West: Post- or Pre-Christian", *First Things* (February 2023), https://www.firstthings.com/article/2023/02/the-west-post--or-pre-christian.

Peter Brown, author of an admirable recent scholarly biography of the saint, credits him with a "highly sophisticated" view of sexuality that makes him, considered in the "harsh moral climate" of his day, a "moderate" with regard to sexuality. "He expected that, ideally, intercourse should take place only to conceive children; but this was no more than austere pagans had demanded. He considered that the extreme views of some Christians, that marriage should be a competition in continence, was not applicable to the average man; and he knew very well that it was positively harmful if used by one partner against the other."[11]

Certainly there is nothing fanatical about these words of the bishop, telling his flock to be "chaste, whether in marriage or in total continence":

> If you haven't got wives, it is permissible for you to marry, but only women who haven't got husbands still alive. Women who haven't got husbands are permitted to marry, but only men who haven't got wives still alive. If you have got wives, don't do anything bad apart from your wives. Give them what you demand from them. They owe faithfulness to you, you owe faithfulness to them. The husband ought to be faithful to his wife, the wife to her husband, both of them to God.[12]

Discussing the importance of the virtue of chastity, Thomistic philosopher Josef Pieper makes the point that it is correctly understood as a particular aspect of the cardinal virtue of prudence—an aspect that "renders one able to perceive reality". Pieper is at pains to emphasize the importance of not taking a too-narrow view of unchastity. An unchaste individual, he writes, "wants above all

[11] Brown, *Augustine of Hippo*, 390.

[12] Sermon 260, in *The Works of Augustine: Essential Sermons*, trans. Edmund Hill, O.P. (Hyde Park, N.Y.: New City Press, 2007), 314.

something for himself; he is distracted by an unobjective 'interest'; his constantly strained will-to-pleasure prevents him from confronting reality with that selfless detachment which alone makes genuine knowledge possible."[13] By contrast, chastity enables the chaste person to see reality; and "to be open to the truth of real things and to live by the truth that one has grasped is the essence of the moral being."[14] Considered this way, it is easy to see why Augustine's decision to throw off the blinders of unchastity and embrace chastity was the turning point of his life.

In many ways, Saint Augustine's world was not so different from our own. Here is how he spoke of it in a sermon to his people near the end of his life: "All this crazy parade and ostentation still at full flood, all these superfluous luxuries and pleasures eagerly awaited, and there's no end or limit to greed. How sick our society becomes in the middle of all this! How much licentious self-indulgence has bubbled up everywhere because of the theaters, the organ, the flutes and the dancers!"[15] Organs and flutes are not much of a problem today, but it is not difficult to think of contemporary equivalents that are.

From this perspective, it is hardly unreasonable to hold that the message of Saint Augustine is desperately needed now. In the midst of the moral pigsty that Western secular culture has largely become, he shines as a champion and exponent of the sixth beatitude: "Blessed are the pure in heart, for they shall see God" (Mt 5:8). And although the fullness of that vision will be realized only in heaven, there is a true sense in which, by faith, the pure in heart begin to see God even in this life. Augustine certainly did.

---

[13] Josef Pieper, *The Four Cardinal Virtues* (New York: Harcourt, Brace and World, 1965), 161.

[14] Ibid., 162.

[15] Sermon 346A, in *Essential Sermons*, 404.

Saint Thomas More

(February 7, 1478–July 6, 1535)

The Lawyer Who Won by Losing

It was only fitting that a distinguished lawyer such as Thomas More faced his life's turning point during a trial. But unlike the other trials in which he had been involved, this time it was More himself who stood accused, with death the certain penalty should he be convicted of the heinous offense of treason against the king who had been his friend and whom he had faithfully served.

Although More by no means welcomed the prospect of dying—in fact, he tried hard to avoid it without doing violence to his conscience—what was at stake in this instance was something far more important than even his life. For if he were to save himself by doing as King Henry VIII demanded, he knew he would be lending his name to an act of schism that threatened, and in fact very nearly accomplished, the destruction of Catholicism in England by severing its tie to the Holy See and the pope. That was something this loyal servant of the king would not do, even though refusing to do it would cost him his life.

"No more might this realm of England refuse obedience to the See of Rome", he patiently told his judges, "than might a child refuse obedience to his own natural father."[1] The verdict, to no one's surprise, and certainly not his own, was guilty.

More's trial was his finest hour—on his part, says Hilaire Belloc, no less than an act of "Heroic Faith"[2]—but it was one for which the preparation had begun years earlier. More was born in London on February 7, 1478, the second of six children of well-to-do parents. After serving as a page in the household of the archbishop of Canterbury, he attended Oxford University and then took up the study of law, following in the footsteps of his father, a successful lawyer. Living at this time near a Carthusian monastery, the young man worshipped with the monks and even gave thought to becoming one of them. Now, too, he started wearing a hair shirt, a practice he would continue the rest of his life.

He began to practice law in 1502, and the following year, he was elected to Parliament. In 1505, he married. He and his wife had four children before she died in 1511. Anxious to have a mother for his children, he quickly married a widow, and although he and his second wife had no children of their own, he welcomed the daughter of his wife's first marriage and also later became the guardian of two young girls.

In these years, along with pursuing a successful career in law and public service, More became associated with an international group of Catholic humanists, advocates of the new intellectual currents of the day, who included the eminent Erasmus of Rotterdam. The two men became fast friends, and it is Erasmus who is generally credited with being the first to call More "a man for all seasons"—a verbal tag that four centuries later became the title of Robert Bolt's

---

[1] From the transcript of More's trial, in Peter Ackroyd, *The Life of Thomas More* (New York: Doubleday, 1997), 397.

[2] Hilaire Belloc, "Saint Thomas More", in *Characters of the Reformation* (London: Sheed and Ward, 1940), 110.

successful 1960 play about More, as well as the film based on it. Along with enthusiasm for the new learning of the early Renaissance, More and Erasmus shared the conviction that the Catholic Church was in urgent need of reform.

Historian Christopher Dawson lists several serious abuses of that day: popes became increasingly involved in the political infighting of the city-states of divided Italy; bishops, who often had more than one diocese, sometimes chose not to reside in any of them, while growing rich on their revenues; and many large abbeys became, in Dawson's words, "primarily great landowning corporations".[3] Martin Luther and others like him had abundant grounds for complaint, although their demands for reform soon passed beyond calling for the elimination of genuine abuses to matters of fundamental doctrine, while they themselves became clients of friendly princes who provided them with patronage and protection.

More's approach, reflecting his interest in the humanism of the day as well as his commitment to reform, is reflected in his famous book *Utopia*. Published in 1516 and written in Latin, the international language of those times, the slim volume became the sixteenth century's equivalent of a bestseller and earned More an international reputation. The interpretative key to *Utopia* (the name is Greek for "no place") is its subtle irony—irony so subtle, in fact, as sometimes to leave today's readers asking, "But does he *really* believe that?" The book describes an imaginary land whose generally admirable principles and practices, though without the benefit of revealed truth, stand in implied contrast with the manifest failings of Christian Europe in the sixteenth century. Within this fictional framework, the

---

[3] Christopher Dawson, *The Dividing of Christendom* (San Francisco: Ignatius Press, 2008), 82–83.

author is at liberty to air views that might otherwise have
landed him in trouble.

Even so, considering later events, the words of a Uto-
pian prayer, as More gives them, seem almost to anticipate
what lay ahead for him: "Grant me an easy death, when
Thou takest me to Thyself. I do not presume to suggest
whether it should be late or soon. But if it is Thy will, I
would much rather come to Thee by a most painful death,
than be kept too long away from Thee by the most pleas-
ant of earthly lives."[4]

Knighted in 1521, More pursued a career that included
important diplomatic missions and service as an adviser
to Henry VIII. In 1529, he succeeded Cardinal Thomas
Wolsey as lord chancellor, the second highest office in the
realm after the monarchy itself.

These were the early years of the Protestant Reformation, and King Henry was then the staunchest of oppo-
nents of the upstart religious movement, thereby earning
the pope's praise as "Defender of the Faith". More moved
vigorously to suppress Protestantism in England, and several Protestants were executed; centuries later, Pope Saint
John Paul II remarked candidly that in this matter More
reflected "the limits of the culture of his time", when it
was taken for granted that, given the opportunity, Catholics and Protestants would turn naturally to the state as
their agent for persecuting one another.[5]

Meanwhile, though, trouble was brewing in a different quarter. Increasingly frustrated at the failure of his
wife, Catherine of Aragon, to bear a son to succeed him,
and now infatuated with a young woman named Anne

---

[4] Thomas More, *Utopia*, trans. Paul Turner (New York: Penguin Books,
1983), 128.

[5] Pope John Paul II, apostolic letter proclaiming Saint Thomas More Patron
of Statesmen and Politicians (October 31, 2000), no. 4.

Boleyn, Henry had set Catherine aside and was seeking an annulment of his marriage to her. Failure in obtaining Rome's approval for this matter of "the King's divorce", as it was called, had already been Wolsey's undoing. Now, seeing that all this was likely to end badly and certain that he could not in good conscience press Henry's case for the "divorce", More resigned his office as lord chancellor in May 1532 and retired to what he trusted would be a tranquil private life.

"Moderation, virtue and good will, honesty, learning, and genius were all unavailing against the dark side of history", a historian remarks.[6] More hoped he had escaped the intrigues and maneuvers of the royal court, but that was not to be. After long delay, Pope Clement VII finally said no to the annulment, and Henry, infuriated, went on a rampage. Having forced Parliament to declare him supreme head of the Church in England, he obtained an enactment requiring the taking of an oath affirming his supremacy and set to work executing those who refused. With the exception of Bishop John Fisher of Rochester, the other active bishops accepted Henry's new ecclesiology. More kept his silence, but he did not take the oath.

Realizing that the silence of so eminent and respected a man was itself an unspoken criticism of his policy, Henry ordered More arrested. On April 17, 1534, Thomas More joined Bishop Fisher in the notorious Tower of London. There he remained for nearly fifteen months, writing, praying, and rejecting repeated overtures—by his family as well as by emissaries of the king—to persuade him to change his mind.

---

[6] Garrett Mattingly, *Catherine of Aragon* (New York: Quality Paperback Books, 1990), 343.

In the spring of 1535, Bishop Fisher, whom the pope
had by then named a cardinal, was tried for treason, convicted, and sentenced to death.[7] On June 22, the emaciated
prelate was awakened at five in the morning and told he
would be executed at nine; asked if he wanted anything,
he said he wished to sleep a bit longer and then dozed until
seven. At nine o'clock, too weak to walk to the scaffold,
he was carried there in a chair, sang the Te Deum ("We
praise you, O God, we acknowledge you to be the Lord"),
and was beheaded. His head was then placed for public
exhibition on London Bridge.

On July 1, Thomas More was taken from his cell and
tried on charges of sedition and insulting King Henry. At
this turning point, he might still have saved himself by
taking the king's oath. Seeing that his condemnation and
death were now certain, he finally spoke his mind:

> This indictment is based upon an act of parliament di-
> rectly repugnant to the laws of God and his holy Church
> whose supreme government in whole or part no tempo-
> ral ruler may presume to take upon himself. That right
> belongs to the See of Rome—a spiritual preeminence
> conferred by our Savior himself and belonging by right
> only to St. Peter and his successors. This realm, being only
> one member and small part of the Church, may not make
> a particular law contrary to the general law of Christ's
> universal Catholic Church.... Necessity alone obliges
> me to say so much in declaring my conscience. But it is
> not so much on account of the supremacy question that
> you seek my blood as because I would not agree to the
> king's marriage.[8]

---

[7] Fisher and More were not the first to die. Shortly before their executions,
three Carthusians, who had also been imprisoned in the Tower, were taken
out and killed.

[8] Ackroyd, *Life of Thomas More*, 397.

As expected, the jury of twelve men speedily pro-
nounced More guilty. Biographer Peter Ackroyd comments, "There is no reason to believe that the jury ...
were overtly persuaded to find the case against More
proven; but if they had declared him innocent, they might
themselves have been imprisoned or even attainted. It was
not a trial which More could have won."[9] He was sentenced to be hanged, disemboweled while still living, and
beheaded. The king "graciously" declared that beheading
would suffice. The execution took place on July 6. More's
last words, spoken to the executioner, were "You will
give me this day a benefit greater than any mortal man
could give me."[10]

Christopher Dawson writes of the deaths of Fisher and
More that "accustomed as men were to acts of violence,
the execution of a Cardinal and a Lord Chancellor, men
who were well known throughout Christendom, for no
crime or theological error, save the refusal of the oath, was
something unheard-of and terrifying."[11] But if Christendom was shaken by these events and others taking place
elsewhere, it was shattered by the bloody wars of religion
that followed all too soon, leaving Europe more divided
than it had been for a millennium and serving only to
prove that, in Dawson's words, "war was no solution of
religious differences".[12]

Henry VIII eventually took six women as wives. Two he
executed, and four he divorced. Belloc gives this disturbing
picture of the king in his later years: "He had become so
huge, unwieldy and corrupt in person that he could hardly
move.... He would express, in the orders he gave, a sort

[9] Ibid., 399.
[10] Ibid., 406.
[11] Dawson, *The Dividing of Christendom*, 117.
[12] Ibid., 179.

of hellish savagery and greed of suffering and gloat over the agonies of his victims."[13] Opinion is divided as to whether Henry suffered from syphilis.

Thomas More and John Fisher were among the first of those several hundred Catholics—priests, laymen, and laywomen—known collectively to history as the English Martyrs. (Protestants also have their English Martyrs, although it is one of the tragedies of history that their faith and the faith of the Catholic martyrs were violently opposed.)

Among the numerous Catholics who died under Queen Elizabeth I, daughter of Henry VIII and Anne Boleyn, was the Jesuit martyr Saint Edmund Campion, subject of a splendid short biography first published in 1935 by Catholic convert and novelist Evelyn Waugh. Near its end, Waugh says something that applies equally well to More, Fisher, and all the rest of those faithful souls. Recalling the dark days of English Catholicism in the eighteenth century, when the Catholic Church did indeed seem near extinction, he writes, "It was then, when the whole gallant sacrifice appeared to have been prodigal and vain, that the story of the martyrs lent them strength. We are the heirs of their conquest, and enjoy, at our ease, the plenty which they died to win."[14]

Saint Teresa of Avila, in her autobiography, shares a delightful anecdote involving her and her brother Rodrigo. An avid reader of stories of martyrs, she decided at the age of eleven or so that she, too, would win immediate entrance into the delights of heaven and then persuaded her brother to join her in seeking martyrdom. "We agreed to go off to

[13] Belloc, "King Henry VIII", in *Characters of the Reformation*, 42.
[14] Evelyn Waugh, *Edmund Campion* (London: Penguin Books, 1954), 167–68.

the country of the Moors ... so that they might behead us", she writes. But an uncle encountered the two children as they were setting out and brought them back home. "Our greatest hindrance seemed to be that we had a father and a mother", the saint records.[15]

Besides illustrating the need to keep an eye on children, even pious ones, the incident points to two other important conclusions. One is that martyrdom is not something to be sought, and thrusting oneself and perhaps others forward to be martyred is reprobated by the Fathers of the Church. The other is that when the crown of martyrdom is offered, it should be accepted. Saint Thomas More exemplifies both points.

Clearly hoping to avoid a confrontation with Henry VIII over the latter's claim to be supreme head of the English Church, More, even after his arrest, was at pains to avoid saying anything that would put him on record in opposition to the king. When his daughter Meg, the favorite among his children, visited him in his cell in the Tower and sought to persuade him to take the oath, as she herself had done, the most More would say was that he had given long thought to the matter—including the "very worst and the uttermost that can possibly happen"—and would not depart from the decision dictated by his conscience. "God makes me a little child and sets me on his lap and dandles me", he told her.[16]

Is there any practical lesson in all this for Catholics of the twenty-first century? Literal martyrdom is plainly not in the cards in the foreseeable future in the United States and other democracies. But, that said, there may be more to this particular matter than one might imagine.

[15] Teresa of Avila, *The Life of Teresa of Avila* (Garden City, N.Y.: Doubleday Image Books, 1960), 60.
[16] Ackroyd, *Life of Thomas More*, 374–75.

Cardinal Francis George, O.M.I., of Chicago quoted himself as once having told a group of priests, "I expect to die in bed, my successor will die in prison and his successor will die a martyr in the public square." Admitting that this was an "overly dramatic" version of what might be expected if society ever became totally secularized, Cardinal George, who died in 2015, nevertheless pointed out that accounts of his words generally left out what he added after speaking of the imaginary martyrdom of a future bishop of Chicago: "His successor will pick up the shards of a ruined society and slowly help rebuild civilization, as the church has done so often in human history."[17]

Martyred bishops to one side, there is no question that the secularizing of society has proceeded apace in the years since Cardinal George made his famous remark and that the more extreme forces of secularization now exhibit an increasingly hostile and aggressive face toward religion, including the Catholic Church. Declaring what is happening to be a "religious revolution", Archbishop Charles J. Chaput, the former archbishop of Philadelphia, writes, "For many generations a common Christian culture transcended our partisan struggles. It gave us a shared framework of behavior and belief. Now another vision for our nation's future has emerged. It sees no need for Christianity. And in many cases it views our faith as an obstacle to its ambitions."[18]

Obviously, in America today, people of faith are not jailed and executed for being believers. But it is by no means

---

[17] Quoted in Tim Drake, "Cardinal George: The Myth and Reality of 'I'll Die in My Bed'", *National Catholic Register*, April 17, 2015, https://www.ncregister.com/blog/cardinal-george-the-myth-and-reality-of-ill-die-in-my-bed.

[18] Charles J. Chaput, *Strangers in a Strange Land* (New York: Henry Holt, 2017), 19.

unusual for them to suffer a kind of "dry" martyrdom via weapons such as discriminatory laws and regulations, as well as private means that include rejecting them for jobs for which they are well qualified, denying them promotions, and turning down their books and articles as being too orthodox to merit publication. The point was made powerfully by Pope John Paul II in his 1993 encyclical on moral principles, *Veritatis Splendor* (*The Splendor of Truth*):

> Although martyrdom represents the high point of the witness to moral truth, and one to which relatively few people are called, there is nonetheless a consistent witness which all Christians must daily be ready to make, even at the cost of suffering and grave sacrifice. Indeed, faced with the many difficulties which fidelity to the moral order can demand, even in the most ordinary circumstances, the Christian is called, with the grace of God invoked in prayer, to a sometimes heroic commitment. In this he or she is sustained by the virtue of fortitude, whereby—as [Pope] Gregory the Great teaches—one can actually "love the difficulties of this world for the sake of eternal rewards".[19]

Thomas More could have testified to the truth of that.

---

[19] John Paul II, encyclical letter *Veritatis Splendor* (August 6, 1993), no. 93.

Saint Ignatius Loyola

(October 23, 1491–July 31, 1556)

Ad majorem Dei gloriam

A Jesuit historian of the last century provides this thumb-nail sketch of Saint Ignatius Loyola: "Basque to the bone, intense, practical, steadfast, un-effusive, completely self-forgetful". In Ignatius, says Father James Brodrick, S.J., "passionate orthodoxy" combined with a "clear-cut vision of human life as a battleground of God and the devil" to produce an extraordinary individual of extraordinary vision and rock-solid determination.[1]

It was God's plan that Ignatius found what Christopher Dawson calls "the most effective instrument for the reform of the Church" in the face of the Protestant Reformation—the Society of Jesus. And although this founding naturally was a complex task, it rested firmly on the bedrock of a small but hugely influential volume composed by the founder—the *Spiritual Exercises*. Of this justly famous book Dawson says, "Here at last men found what they had been looking for—a new approach to the problem of reform, a reformation which started at the center and transformed the personality."[2]

[1] James Brodrick, S.J., *The Origins of the Jesuits* (Chicago: Loyola Press, 1997), 1.

[2] Christopher Dawson, *The Dividing of Christendom* (San Francisco: Ignatius Press, 2008), 152.

Such transformation was, in fact, something that Ignatius himself had experienced, although in his case it took much longer than the mere thirty days that the *Exercises* took and was far more arduous.

Ignatius was born on October 23, 1491—eight years after Martin Luther, in the same year as King Henry VIII of England, and less than a year before Columbus reached the New World. His family belonged to the minor nobility of the Basque Country of northern Spain whose traditional occupation was soldiering. As a teenager, the youth became a page in the royal court of Castile, where he busied himself for the decade that followed in what his priest secretary—no doubt using Ignatius' own words—calls "gaming, affairs with women, dueling, and armed affrays".[3]

The divine intervention that marks a turning point in many lives can take various forms. Sometimes it is a single dramatic event, such as Saint Paul's encounter with the risen Jesus on the road to Damascus. Sometimes it is the culmination of a process extending over months or even years—think of Saint Augustine. And sometimes it is a combination of both—a dramatic event followed by a lengthy process. The conversion of Ignatius Loyola from courtier and soldier to the founder of the Jesuits was of that third kind, beginning with a serious injury, continuing through long months of recovery, and culminating in a turning point at a place called Manresa.

The events leading up to it were unremarkable for a young man of his time, place, and background. Following the death of the royal official who was his patron, he had joined the army of the viceroy of Navarre. The spring of 1521 found him commanding the outnumbered,

---

[3] Quoted in Mary Purcell, *The First Jesuit* (Garden City, N.Y.: Image Books, 1965), 37.

outgunned Spanish defenders of the city of Pamplona, then under siege by a French army during one of the petty wars of that day. Ignatius fought valiantly until a cannonball shattered his right leg. Admiring his courage, the victorious French transported him by litter to his family's castle. And there, lying in an upper room, he suffered alternately from physical pain—the damaged leg had to be reset, an excruciating procedure, performed without anesthesia, that left him with a permanent limp—and from the agonies of boredom.

Before his injury, Ignatius had enjoyed reading romantic tales of knighthood and chivalry, but the only books in the castle were about the life of Christ and a volume of saints' lives. As he read these, he began wondering, "How would it be if I did this thing that Saint Francis did or what Saint Dominic did?" One night, he had a vision of the Blessed Virgin and the Child Jesus that moved him to feel disgust with his unruly life and resolve to make a pilgrimage to Jerusalem.

First, though, he went to the great Marian shrine at Montserrat. He intended to stay only a few days but remained for months while experiencing deepening spiritual illumination and undergoing a profound change of life. Having made a general confession, Ignatius, the courtier and soldier who had worn the proud livery of elegance, gave away his fine clothes, dressed in rags, begged for alms, and lived with the poor. Outside the nearby town of Manresa, he found an isolated cave in which he spent time praying and meditating. Now, for the first time, he read Thomas à Kempis' classic, *The Imitation of Christ*, and was deeply influenced by it. Here, too, he was inspired to begin thinking of some sort of spiritual militia committed to God's service and began to compose the volume that was to become the *Spiritual Exercises*.

The turning point for Ignatius was a great "illumination of spirit" that came to him as he sat on the bank of the nearby Cardoner River. Much later, his biographer described it like this: "It was not a vision, but understanding and knowledge of many things, some concerning spiritual things, others concerning faith and human learning.... All the helps God gave him during his whole life, together with everything he himself learned in his sixty-two years on earth, was less than the graces he received that day sitting by the river. Moreover, this enlightenment remained with him so that he seemed to himself afterward a different man, possessed of a new intellect."[4] In later years, when early members of the Society of Jesus questioned him about the source of this or that aspect of the group's way of life, the founder responded simply, "Manresa".

After many delays and disappointments, Ignatius finally managed to reach Jerusalem, but the Franciscans who were responsible for pilgrims refused to let him stay, fearing that his zeal for preaching the gospel to the Muslims, who were in control there, would lead to trouble. Upon returning to Spain, aware by now that to serve the Lord well he would need more than the rudimentary education he possessed, Ignatius settled down to studies—first, among schoolboys, with the object of learning Latin; then at the University of Salamanca; and finally, with the aim of studying theology, at the renowned University of Paris, where he eventually received a master of arts degree.

While there, Ignatius began attracting companions and disciples, among them Francis Xavier and Peter Faber, both destined to be canonized. For their formation he made use of the *Spiritual Exercises*. The slim volume, which still provides the basis for Ignatian retreats, is not a devotional

---

[4] From the documents of his canonization, quoted in ibid., 111.

work and can make for dry reading for those who do not
realize its purpose. It is a manual for retreat masters, setting
out the stages intended to lead retreatants to make a firm
commitment to the service of God. Its spirit is obvious
in the "Principle and Foundation" with which it begins:
"Man is created to praise, reverence, and serve God, our
Lord, and by this means to save his soul. All other things
on the face of the earth are created for man to help him
fulfill the end for which he is created.... Man is to use
these things to the extent they will help him to attain his
end. Likewise, he must rid himself of them in so far as they
prevent him from attaining it."[5]

Regarding the intended audience of the *Exercises*,
theologian Robert W. Gleason, S.J., writes that although
directed to "many classes of people", they are intended
especially for "*more* generous souls from whom *greater*
service and love of God might be hoped". The aim, he
adds, is "an apostolic spirit of generous service, a life of
sanctity penetrated by prayer and supporting and evok-
ing it, rather than a spirituality purely contemplative or
mystical in its orientation".[6] Ultimately, the *Exercises* seek
one great outcome: the greater glory of God. (*Ad majorem
Dei gloriam*—"To the greater glory of God"—is the motto
of the Jesuits.) Throughout, says Christopher Dawson,
"there is little theology, and no intellectual discussion. It
is a direct appeal to the will, based on one spiritual axiom,
and to the imagination stimulated by the contemplation of
the life of Christ. But this was sufficient to change men's
lives and to bring about far-reaching changes in society
and culture."[7]

[5] *The Spiritual Exercises of St. Ignatius*, trans. Anthony Mottola (Garden City,
N.Y.: Doubleday Image Books, 1964), 47.

[6] Ibid., 21.

[7] Dawson, *Dividing of Christendom*, 150.

Following a Mass celebrated in a small chapel on the slope of Montmartre on August 15, 1534—the feast of the Blessed Virgin Mary's Assumption into heaven—Ignatius and six others made a joint vow committing themselves to the service of God. This was the beginning of the Society of Jesus (although, as yet, the group had no name). In 1537, the small band made its way to Rome and there received the encouragement of Pope Paul III. The pope's formal approval was forthcoming in 1540, and at that time Ignatius was chosen superior general for life.

From the start, the Society was a novelty. Unlike other religious orders, the Jesuits did not recite the office together in choir. To the traditional three vows of poverty, chastity, and obedience they added a fourth vow of loyalty to the pope, pledging to go wherever he sent them and do whatever work he assigned. Says Dawson, "All external rules and practices were reduced by [Ignatius] to a minimum. Everything was designed to make the Society as flexible and as united as possible, so that it would be free to turn its energies in whatever direction they were needed."[8]

The Jesuits grew rapidly in numbers and spread throughout Europe and then to the Americas and, via Francis Xavier, to the Far East. They established schools, becoming renowned as educators, had important roles in the reforming Council of Trent, wrote catechisms (notably Saint Peter Canisius in Germany), preached and served as confessors and spiritual guides, and everywhere gave retreats based on the *Spiritual Exercises*. Although by no means the only force driving the Catholic Renewal, the Jesuits spearheaded this revival of Catholicism in response to the challenge of militant Protestantism. Hilaire Belloc, writing with his customary gusto at a time before ecumenical sensitivities softened the

[8] Ibid., 153.

rhetoric employed when these matters are discussed, offered this explanation for the "sweeping success" of the early Jesuits: "The new fighting force of the Catholic Church had stiffening it, as armies have, a certain *morale*. It insisted upon things essential to the moment and to the combat: personal rectitude and learning. It turned the scale of discussion, putting all the best weapons into Catholic hands."[9]

Now Ignatius lived in Rome, from which he supervised all this as it took shape. Writers commonly make much of the military side of Ignatius, and it is certainly visible in the disciplined style he imposed on the Society, reflected in his writing of its constitution (which was not finally approved until two years after his death). Busy as he was, however, says the Jesuit poet Gerard Manley Hopkins, he regarded personal fame as "the most dangerous and dazzling of all attractions" and lived "so ordinary, so hidden a life, that when after his death they began to move in the process of his canonization one of the cardinals, who had known him in his later life ... said that he had never remarked anything in him more than in any edifying priest."[10]

The end came for him on July 31, 1556. By then, the Jesuits, now numbering a thousand, were engaged in a dazzling variety of activities under his direction. But if Ignatius was a general, he was a kindly, even paternal one; among his last acts was to write a young Jesuit a fatherly letter encouraging him to persevere in his vocation.

Five centuries later, an American Jesuit, Father John LaFarge, wrote of Saint Ignatius Loyola that, thanks to the lessons of the spirit that he had learned in "the School of

---

[9] Hilaire Belloc, *How the Reformation Happened* (New York: Robert M. McBride, 1928), 224.

[10] Letter to R. W. Dixon, December 1, 1881, in *A Hopkins Reader*, ed. John Pick (New York: Oxford University Press, 1953), 289. Hopkins was explaining his reluctance to have his poems published in his lifetime.

Manresa", he was "supremely fitted to guide, and teach countless others to guide, the human heart and will in the desperate struggle for decision, in the effective rejection of evil and total embracing of the good".[11] But it is Ignatius himself who gives the best formulation of this "decision" in a famous prayer embodied in the "Contemplation for Obtaining Love of God", which is the heart of the final chapter of the *Spiritual Exercises*: "Take, O Lord, and receive all my liberty, my memory, my understanding, and all my will, all I have and possess. Thou hast given it all to me; to Thee, O Lord, I restore it: all is Thine; dispose of it according to Thy will. Give me Thy love and Thy grace, for this is enough for me."[12]

For a long time, the renewal of the Catholic Church that began in earnest in the sixteenth century was commonly called the Counter-Reformation, but more recently, "Catholic Reform" and "Catholic Renewal" have been the preferred terms. The change is desirable inasmuch as referring to what took place as the *Counter*-Reformation suggests mere opposition—in this case, to the rise and spread of Protestantism. And while Catholicism's reform and renewal were certainly in opposition to Protestantism, the movement was underway well before Martin Luther nailed his Ninety-Five Theses to the church door on October 31, 1517 (the date traditionally considered the start of the Protestant Reformation) and was far more sweeping and positive in both intention and result than the negative characterization would suggest.

[11] John LaFarge, S.J., foreword to *The First Jesuit*, 10.
[12] *Spiritual Exercises*, 104.

It is a fact, however, that internal resistance as well as external opposition made the Catholic Renewal slow to gain traction. Not until 1545 did Pope Paul III finally summon a long-discussed general council to meet in the northern Italian city of Trent, and even then, attendance at its first session was, in Dawson's words, "pitiably small"—a mere fifty-one bishops. Participation improved after that, although it was mostly Italian and Spanish bishops who attended. The council continued through two more sessions, in 1551 and 1561–1563, concluding under Pope Pius IV.

In the end, Trent's achievements were significant and covered many areas of Church life. For example, regarding governance, bishops were no longer to be ordinaries of more than one diocese at a time and were required to live in their dioceses, as a significant number had been accustomed not to do up to then; and regarding the formation of priests, every diocese was to have a seminary. Various abusive practices—such as nepotism, the awarding of Church offices and their income to members of one's family, with little or no regard to their qualifications—were ordered to cease. In addition, steps were taken toward doctrinal clarification, notably including a mandate for a new universal catechism: the Roman Catechism, commonly known as the Catechism of the Council of Trent; it was published by Pope Saint Pius V in 1566 and remained the Church's universal catechism until the *Catechism of the Catholic Church*, prepared at the direction of Pope Saint John Paul II, was published in 1992.

Several Jesuits were active at Trent, including Father Diego Laynez, Saint Ignatius' first successor as general of the Society, but Ignatius himself did not live to see the council's conclusion. Beyond question, however, Ignatius was a towering figure in the work of Catholic reform and renewal that Trent put in place. He had grasped the need much earlier—during his years at the University of Paris, when, it is said, he first came face-to-face with the challenge to the Church presented by the new, aggressive Protestantism of the day. As the Council of Trent moved ahead, Ignatius was bringing to completion the *Spiritual Exercises*, and to that powerful instrument of renewal he now added its final substantial piece—a relatively short document called "Rules for Thinking with the Church".[13]

"In order to have the proper attitude of mind in the Church Militant", he wrote, "we should observe the following rules." Then follow a set of propositions whose thrust is clear from the start: "Putting aside all private judgment, we should keep our minds prepared and ready to obey promptly in all things the true spouse of Christ our Lord, our Holy Mother, the hierarchical Church." This is followed by a list of things to be valued and affirmed: sacramental confession of sins, the Mass, the religious life, priestly celibacy, saints' relics, and fasting and abstinence at designated times. It is necessary, Ignatius declared, "to praise all the precepts of the Church, holding ourselves ready at all times to find reasons for their defense, and never offending against them".

Some readers express consternation at the thirteenth proposition on Ignatius' list of rules, which reads in part, "I will believe that the white that I see is black, if the hierarchical Church so defines it." Leaving aside the element of exaggeration in order to make a point, it is clear that his intent was to assert that individual human perception, always fallible, must cede to the solemn teaching of the infallible Church: "For the same Spirit and Lord, who gave us the Ten Commandments, guides and governs our Holy Mother Church", Ignatius explains.

---

[13] *Spiritual Exercises*, 139–42.

Today we live in an era not unlike the sixteenth century—a time of rapid change and uncertainty, when old verities are often challenged and confusion is widespread. This also is a postconciliar era, the period following the Second Vatican Council, whose impact is sometimes compared to Trent's. Time will tell whether the comparison is appropriate. But it is a fact that Vatican II, rather than making a sharp break with the past, as sometimes is claimed, built upon and developed what came before it, including the achievement of Trent and the Catholic Renewal.

Pope Benedict XVI, who as a young theologian was much involved in Vatican II, emphasized that point in an address in which he spoke of two ways of interpreting the council: the "hermeneutic of discontinuity and rupture" and the "hermeneutic of reform". It is this second way— the way of reform—that is correct, he insisted, and that results in "innovation in continuity", the source of "new life ... and new fruit".[14] Saint Ignatius Loyola was many things, but in a special way, he represented the hermeneutic of reform at work in the Church of his day.

[14] Pope Benedict XVI, Address to the Roman Curia, December 22, 2005.

Saint Benedict Joseph Labre

(March 26, 1748–April 16, 1783)

He Took the World as His Monastery

As might be expected, God frequently raises up saints who are especially well suited to the particular needs of their times. Think of Paul the Apostle, whose zeal and high intelligence equipped him to keep Christianity from becoming a marginalized Jewish sect by preaching Christ's gospel to the Gentile world, or of Pope Saint John Paul II, whose lofty intellect and inspiring leadership placed him providentially at the head of the Church just as Soviet Communism was losing its grip on Eastern Europe.

Somewhat surprisingly, though, God seems at other times to show no less preference for saints who stand conspicuously apart from the secular currents of their times. Perhaps his intention in these cases is to remind us that, measured by the scale of eternity, the issues exercising us here and now do not matter as much as we are tempted to imagine.

Benedict Joseph Labre clearly was this second kind of saint.

He was certainly unusual. Historian James Hitchcock calls him "one of the strangest saints in the history of the Church".[1] Not a martyr or a missionary, neither theologian

---

[1] James Hitchcock, *History of the Catholic Church* (San Francisco: Ignatius Press, 2012), 323.

nor cloistered religious, in an era when skepticism was much in vogue, he chose to be a homeless vagabond who, having spent years on perpetual pilgrimage to the great shrines of Europe, died finally of malnutrition after living as a street person in Rome.

His short life occupied the latter years of the eighteenth century, during the high tide of the Enlightenment, the rationalist movement that, preaching secularist dogma in opposition to supernatural faith, spread from France throughout much of Europe and as far as the New World. Its principal spokesman was François-Marie Arouet (1694–1778)—better known by his pen name, Voltaire—a brilliant propagandist famed for the slogan *Ecrasez l'infame*, "Crush the infamous one", by which he meant the Catholic Church.

"The aim of the Enlightenment", says Hitchcock, "was not toleration but the replacement of one kind of orthodoxy by another, demanding liberation from political and religious authority but by no means espousing complete freedom of expression."[2] The movement had its own version of religion—Deism or "natural religion"—which considered God to be a kind of divine clockmaker who designed the world and set it ticking but thereafter left it to its own devices. This natural religion even crossed the ocean to the American colonies, where Thomas Jefferson, a faithful Deist, produced a cut-and-paste version of the Gospels from which he had scrupulously eliminated any mention of Jesus' miracles and the Resurrection. Although they did not know it, Voltaire and his colleagues were helping set the scene for the French Revolution a few years later, including its trademark killing machine, the guillotine.

This, then, was the setting into which, on March 26, 1748, in the town of Amettes in northern France, the future

[2] Ibid., 328.

saint was born, the first of fifteen children of a well-to-do
shopkeeper named Jean-Baptiste Labre and his wife,
Anne-Barba. The boy proved to be a quiet, thoughtful
child whose family supposed him to have a calling to the
priesthood. With the intention of preparing him for that,
his parents sent him when he was twelve to live with his
paternal uncle Father François-Joseph Labre, parish priest
in the nearby town of Érin.

Although the boy made progress under his uncle's tute-
lage and Benedict loved reading Scripture, he was increasingly uninterested in formal studies and attracted only
to what had to do with the contemplation of God. As
time passed, the idea grew in him that he would become
a Trappist. But his parents said no—he was too young.
Then a plague broke out in the town, and his uncle died
while tending the sick. Benedict returned home still bent
on a monastic life, and his parents, by now convinced that
this really was the will of God, gave their approval. But
another priest uncle suggested the Carthusians rather than
the Trappists, and Benedict, now eighteen, set off to realize his dream.

Doing that nevertheless proved not so easy. The Trappists said no to him. So did two Carthusian monasteries, with the second pointing out that before it could
accept him, he would have to learn plainchant and logic.
Returning home, he did as he had been directed and then
set out again on his quest. He lasted only six weeks as a
postulant with the Carthusians, however. Undaunted,
Benedict wrote his parents: "Give me your blessing, and I
will never again be a cause of trouble to you. I very much
hope to be received at La Trappe [the Trappist monastery where he was rejected before]; but if I should fail
there, I am told that at the Abbey of Sept Fons [another
Trappist monastery] they are less severe, and will receive

candidates like me. But I think I shall be received at
La Trappe."[3]

Wrong again. So now it was off to Sept Fons. Admitted finally to that Trappist abbey, he stayed for all of eight
months, impressing the community by his humility and
exactness in observing the rule, until his health gave way
under the pressure of extreme fasting and penances rashly
imposed by himself far beyond what the rule required.
After he had spent time recovering in the abbey's infirmary, the monks, having reached the reasonable conclusion that he was not called to the disciplined Trappist life,
asked him to leave.

And so Benedict found himself once more at loose ends
in the world. This prompted another letter to his parents.
Dated August 31, 1770, it is worth quoting for the light it
sheds on his state of mind at the time:

> My dear Father and Mother,
>   You have heard that I have left the Abbey of Sept
> Fons, and no doubt you are uneasy and desirous to know
> what route I have taken, and what kind of life I intend
> to adopt. I must therefore acquaint you that I left Sept
> Fons in July; I had a fever soon after I left, which lasted
> four days, and I am now on my way to Rome. I have not
> traveled very fast since I left, on account of the excessive
> hot weather there always is in the month of August in
> Piedmont, where I now am, and where, on account of a
> little complaint, I have been detained for three weeks in
> a hospital where I was kindly treated. In other respects I
> have been very well.
>   There are in Italy many monasteries where the religious
> live very regular and austere lives; I design to enter into
> one of them, and I hope that God will prosper my design.

[3] Quoted in Archbishop Alban Goodier, S.J., *Saints for Sinners* (Freeport,
N.Y.: Books for Libraries Press, 1970), 185–86.

Do not make yourselves uneasy on my account. I will not fail to write to you from time to time. And I shall be glad to hear of you, and of my brothers and sisters; but this is not possible at present, because I am not yet settled in any fixed place; I will not fail to pray for you every day. I beg that you will pardon me for all the uneasiness that I have given you; and that you will give me your blessing, that God may favor my design....

Your most affectionate son,
Benedict Joseph Labre[4]

This was the last letter he is known to have written his parents.

His hopes for admission to another monastery were, of course, disappointed. But by now another idea had begun to dawn on him—the understanding of what he believed God was really asking of him. Archbishop Alban Goodier, S.J., explains this turning point: "He could not live in the confinement of a monastery; then the whole world should be his cloister. There he would live, a lonely life with God, the loneliest of lonely men.... He would be a tramp, God's own poor man, depending on whatever men gave him from day to day, a pilgrim to heaven for the remainder of his life."[5]

This was a way of life whose first period was to last the next six or seven years. Now Benedict lived the life of a perpetual pilgrim, plodding steadily among the great shrines and holy places of Western Europe—Rome, Loreto, Assisi, Einsiedeln, Paray-le-Monial, Santiago de Compostela, and others. He went on foot, begging for food and sleeping where he could—often outdoors and, on one occasion, at the farm belonging to the parents of the future Curé of Ars, Saint John Vianney.

[4] Quoted in ibid., 189–91.
[5] Ibid., 187–88.

He spoke little and, when opportunity presented itself, spent long hours in prayer before the Blessed Sacrament. He wore an old coat, had a rosary around his neck and another between his fingers, kept his arms folded over a crucifix on his chest, and carried a small satchel that contained only a Bible, a breviary, *The Imitation of Christ*, and a few other religious books.

After enduring years of this self-imposed regimen on the road, he finally settled—after his own fashion—in Rome, and there he remained until his death, except for an annual visit to the Holy House of Loreto, said to be the dwelling where Mary received the Annunciation and the Holy Family lived during their years in Nazareth. In Rome, he slept in a cranny in the ruins of the Colosseum and spent his days visiting the city's churches, especially—a practice that later earned him the title "Saint of the Blessed Sacrament"— any church where the eucharistic devotion called the Forty Hours was taking place. He lived on alms (when people thought to give them) and otherwise subsisted on scraps rescued from the trash.

The priest who became his confessor and eventually his biographer left this description of him in those latter days: "In the month of June, 1782, just after I had celebrated Mass ... I noticed a man close beside me whose appearance at first sight was decidedly unpleasant and forbidding. His legs were only partially covered, his clothes were tied around his waist with an old cord. His hair was uncombed, he was ill-clad, and wrapped about in an old and ragged coat. In his outward appearance he seemed to be the most miserable beggar I had ever seen."[6]

Even so, the painter Antonio Cavallucci saw enough in Benedict's appearance to paint him twice and even use

---

[6] Ibid., 194–95.

him as a model for Christ. The portraits depict a thin, bearded young man with downcast eyes, apparently lost in thought—or prayer.

On April 15, 1783, Benedict collapsed outside a church and was carried to a nearby house, where he died the next day of malnutrition. He was thirty-five. As word of his death spread, his confessor recalled, "all at once the little children from the houses hard by filled the whole street with their noise, crying out with one accord, 'The Saint is dead, the Saint is dead.'"[7]

Soon the whole city was saying the same thing. Many holy people before him had died in Rome, his biographer remarked, "but the death of none of them ever excited so rapid and lively an emotion ... as the death of this poor beggar".[8] Great crowds came to view his body lying in state in a church near the Colosseum, and there beside the main altar he was buried on Easter Sunday afternoon.

After Benedict's death, many miracles were reported as having been worked through his intercession. Blessed Pius IX beatified him in 1860. Pope Leo XIII called him "holiness itself" when canonizing him in 1881. Writing of his holiness, Archbishop Goodier says the first thought of anyone who looks into his story has to be "There is no condition of life which the grace of God has not sanctified." And he adds, "Rousseau and Voltaire had died five years before; ten years later came the execution of Louis XVI, and the massacres of the French Revolution were at their height. In studying the life of Benedict Joseph Labre these dates cannot be without their significance."[9]

Taken as a whole, his way of life is no model for imitation by anybody, yet his fidelity to the calling he believed

[7] Ibid., 198.
[8] Ibid.
[9] Ibid., 177–78.

he had received was heroic, his devotion to the Blessed Sacrament was indeed exemplary, and his total indifference to the rationalism and skepticism of his time was admirable. No one has taken more literally Jesus' instructions to trust in God and not be anxious about food, drink, and clothing (see Mt 6:31). And in its own inimitable manner, his life mirrors Paul's advice to all who wish to be Christ's disciples: "Set your minds on things that are above, not on things that are on earth. For you have died, and your life is hidden with Christ in God" (Col 3:2–3).

People of religious faith should be careful not to romanticize poverty. As the vast majority of those who have poverty thrust upon them experience it, material poverty is a soul-deadening experience involving ill-health, bad housing and bad schools, widespread sexual immorality, abortion, the abuse of drugs and alcohol, and the daily threats that come with life in a crime-ridden neighborhood. People of faith fortunate enough not to be poor should do all they can to eradicate poverty while helping their brothers and sisters in need.

At the same time, saying this in no way reduces the importance of the voluntary practice of poverty chosen as an ascetical tool for growing in the love of God. Saint Benedict Joseph Labre was a member of the Third Order of Saint Francis, and for him, the special attraction of the saint of Assisi very likely lay in Francis' practice of poverty. For Saint Francis, poverty was a path to freedom— detachment from cloying impediments that stand in the way to God. As G.K. Chesterton explains, "You could not threaten to starve a man who was ever striving to fast.

You could not ruin him and reduce him to beggary, for he was already a beggar."[10]

True enough. But there is something more to be said about poverty as saints such as Francis of Assisi and Benedict Joseph Labre embraced it. As William James puts it, "Throughout the annals of the saintly life, we find this ever-recurring note: Fling yourself upon God's providence without making any reserve whatever—take no thought for the morrow—sell all you have and give it to the poor—only when the sacrifice is ruthless and reckless will the higher safety really arrive."[11] In their practice of poverty, Benedict Joseph Labre, Francis of Assisi, and other such holy souls became masters of this art of throwing themselves on God's providence.

Bear in mind, too, that, unusual as it was, the way of life of a pilgrim that Benedict Joseph chose for himself did have precedents. "God's folk" were pilgrims who spent months, years, even their entire lives visiting shrines and receiving hospitality along the way. Tolstoy's *War and Peace* contains a brief episode in which the pious Princess Mary Bolkónskaya is shown tending to several of them. Mary's brother Prince Andrew Bolkónski and his friend Pierre Bezúkhov tease an old woman named Pelagéya, making her feel "frightened and ashamed to have accepted charity at a house where such things could be said" and moving Mary to scold the men until they apologize meekly.[12]

But when all is said and done, was Saint Benedict Joseph out of his mind? While some people think he was,

[10] *Saint Francis of Assisi*, in *The Collected Works of G. K. Chesterton*, vol. 2 (San Francisco: Ignatius Press, 1986), 94.

[11] William James, *The Varieties of Religious Experience* (New York: Longmans, Green, 1929), 321.

[12] *War and Peace*, trans. Louise and Aylmer Maude (New York: Heritage Press, 1938), 517–21.

I believe the truth is more complicated. He was certainly eccentric, and his practice of penance and self-denial went to extremes that no reasonable person would commend to anyone else. But insane? Who can say what illuminations he received during those long hours of contemplation before the Blessed Sacrament, which he so cherished? By the end, his mind may indeed have been affected by illness and physical debilitation, but that is not madness. And before passing judgment on Benedict Joseph Labre, we ought to recall that we live at a time when perversities of all kinds, infanticide, and threatening nuclear warfare all pass for "normal" behavior.

There is something to be learned here from the explanation Flannery O'Connor gave one of her many correspondents who asked why she called her second novel *The Violent Bear It Away* (her own translation of Matthew 11:12, which speaks of those who force their way into the kingdom of heaven). This was her answer: "The violent in this case are the people who are willing to act upon their faith and act vigorously. St. Augustine and St. Thomas say the violent here are ascetics. Anyway it is the kind of passion for the things of God which makes asceticism possible, which puts nothing in the way and lets nothing interfere with winning heaven.... Call it a single-minded assault upon the kingdom of heaven, often accomplished in part by self-denial. By doing the will of God."[13]

If you accept O'Connor's definition, Saint Benedict Joseph Labre is perhaps best understood as one of the violent ones. But there is another account that may suit him even better. Among the few items that he took with

---

[13] Letter to La Trelle, in *Good Things Out of Nazareth: The Uncollected Letters of Flannery O'Connor and Friends*, ed. Benjamin B. Alexander (New York: Convergent, 2019), 255.

him on his solitary pilgrimages was a copy of the spiritual classic *The Imitation of Christ*, and there he will have read and presumably taken to heart this passage: "Blessed is the man who for you, O Lord, abandons all things created; who offers violence to nature and through fervor of spirit crucifies the concupiscence of the flesh: that so, with a serene conscience, he may offer to you pure prayer and become worthy to be admitted among the choirs of angels, having excluded himself both exteriorly and interiorly from all things of earth."[14] Wasn't this the plan of life of that oddest of saints, Benedict Joseph Labre?

[14] Thomas à Kempis, *The Imitation of Christ*, bk. 3, chap. 48.

Saint John Henry Newman

(February 21, 1801–August 11, 1890)

"I Was Denounced as a Traitor"

In his spiritual and intellectual autobiography, the *Apologia pro Vita Sua*, Saint John Henry Newman records the great turning point of his life in this precise, surprisingly laconic manner: "I had begun my *Essay on the Development of Doctrine* at the beginning of 1845, and I was hard at it all through the year till October. As I advanced, my difficulties so cleared away that I ceased to speak of 'the Roman Catholics,' and boldly called them Catholics. Before I got to the end, I resolved to be received."[1] A few days later, he entered the Catholic Church. The *Apologia*, needless to say, tells the story of his conversion at much greater length.

Newman is regarded as one of the most important Catholic theologians of modern times, a thinker whose ideas had, among other things, a major influence on the Second Vatican Council. His *Apologia* occupies a place of honor alongside Saint Augustine's *Confessions* as an account of a spiritual journey. Yet for all that, and by no means unrelated to it, Newman's long life was marked by repeated conflicts and controversies. And despite the unruffled blandness of

[1] John Henry Newman, *Apologia pro Vita Sua: Being a History of His Religious Opinions*, ed. Charles Frederick Harrold (New York: Longmans, Green, 1947), 212.

the account just quoted, suggesting that his decision to "be received" was simple and trouble free, Newman's conversion was considerably more controversial and its consequences more contentious than he lets on.

He was born in London on February 21, 1801, the eldest in a family of three sons and three daughters. His father, John, was a banker, and his mother, Jemima, was a descendant of Protestant Huguenot refugees from France. Raised an Anglican, at the age of fifteen he had a conversion experience—the "beginning of divine faith in me"—that included the inner conviction that he was "predestined to salvation". Although he later abandoned the "detestable" doctrine of predestination, the experience, along with his reading, moved him to embrace an evangelical form of Christianity with a Calvinist tinge.[2]

Newman studied at Oxford, was elected a fellow of Oriel College in April 1822, and in 1825 was ordained an Anglican priest. Several years later, he and several friends launched what came to be called the Oxford Movement. This was a loosely organized group of reform-minded Anglicans who sought to move the Church of England to adopt doctrine and liturgy tending in a more Catholic direction. Seeking a "middle way" between Protestantism and Catholicism, Newman hoped that Anglicanism, reformed along the lines he and his friends were advocating, would play that role.

With this end in view, he organized and helped write a series of pamphlets that he called Tracts for the Times. The Oxford Movement and the tracts flourished between 1833 and 1841, becoming the focus of intense interest and occasional controversy. Ninety tracts were published, with

[2] Ibid., 3–5.

Newman writing about a third of them. But then came his
Tract 90—and everything changed.

In this document, Newman argued that the famous
Thirty-Nine Articles—the crucial sixteenth-century state-
ment of the fundamental beliefs of Anglicanism—did not
criticize the doctrines of the Catholic Church as they had
been taught by the Council of Trent, the great Catholic
reforming council of that era, but merely took exception
to certain popular errors of the day, some of them toler-
ated but not formally adopted by Rome. And if that was
so, readers were quick to understand, then Newman was
saying, in effect, that the crucial founding document of
the Anglican Church had implicitly endorsed the solemn
teaching of the Catholic Church.

An uproar followed. "I was denounced as a traitor",
Newman recalled.[3] The Anglican bishop of Oxford ordered
that publication of the Tracts for the Times be halted. Newman withdrew from the controversy and settled into a life of
study and prayer at Littlemore, a village near Oxford. Some
people say that, for all practical purposes, his Anglican allegiance ended then, but he saw it differently inasmuch as he
was still wrestling with obstacles that, to his mind, stood in
the way of his becoming a Catholic. These, he concluded,
were largely historical in nature and concerned the fact—if
fact it was—that the Catholic Church in the nineteenth
century taught things that Jesus and the apostles and the
Church Fathers had not taught. And if that was the case,
how could the Catholic Church as she was now claim to be
in continuity with—indeed, substantially the same as—the
Church of apostolic times?

Here, then, was the question that Newman, steeped
in the history of early Christianity as he was, now went
to work to puzzle out. The product of his research and

---

[3] Ibid., 81.

reflection was *An Essay on the Development of Christian Doctrine*. At its start, the author states the "assumption" that he proposes to test in the book: "that the Christianity of the second, fourth, twelfth, sixteenth, and intermediate centuries is in its substance the very religion which Christ and His Apostles taught in the first, whatever may be the modifications for good or for evil which lapse of years, or the vicissitudes of human affairs, have impressed upon it".[4]

That changes in the teaching had occurred was obvious. But Newman found these to be developments of things present in the Church's belief and teaching from the very start. Now, though, rather than simply leave this as an assertion, a conclusion drawn from his own research, Newman carefully demonstrated how development had taken place in numerous specific cases—papal authority, the Immaculate Conception, the canonical books of the New Testament, the two natures in Christ, infant baptism, and much else besides.

He also made it clear that the idea of development was not a blank check to authorize just any sort of change. Rather, he insisted, certain conditions—which he spelled out—had to be met to authenticate anything put forward as a development. Above all, he wrote, "a development, to be faithful, must retain both the doctrine and the principle with which it started."[5] The idea of doctrinal development was hardly new, and others before and since have written on the subject, but Newman's working out of the idea remains an important contribution.

So now, finally, his doubts and hesitations had been resolved. In a postscript to the introduction of the first edition of the *Development of Doctrine*, referring to himself

---

[4] John Henry Newman, *An Essay on the Development of Christian Doctrine* (Garden City, N.Y.: Doubleday Image Books, 1960), 33.

[5] Ibid., 185.

in the third person, he notes that the author had become a Catholic and then adds this: "It was his intention and wish to have carried his volume through the press before deciding finally on this step. But he recognized in himself a conviction of the truth of the conclusion to which the discussion leads so clear as to supersede further deliberation. Shortly afterwards circumstances gave him the opportunity of acting upon it, and he felt that he had no warrant for refusing to do so."[6]

Noting that four of Newman's companions had already left to become Catholics, biographer Ian Ker calls this "not just the right time but the providential time to make the final break".[7] On October 9, 1845, Newman was received into the Catholic Church by Father Dominic Barberi, an Italian Passionist priest who had lately done the same for a friend of Newman's. One long journey had ended, and another had begun. Several months after becoming a Catholic, he traveled to Rome, and there he was ordained a priest and joined Saint Philip Neri's priestly society, the Oratorians. Returning to England, he established the Oratory in London and then in Birmingham, where he made his home.

His career after that had its ups and downs. In 1851, at the invitation of the Irish bishops, he went to Dublin as first rector of the newly established Catholic University—which still exists under the name University College—but Newman and the bishops did not see eye to eye about operating a university, and after several years he returned to England.

One lasting product of this episode, however, was a series of lectures brought together as a book with the title

[6] Ibid., 28.
[7] Ian Ker, *John Henry Newman: A Biography* (Oxford: Oxford University Press, 1990), 316.

The Idea of the University. It is well worth reading today, when many schools profess at best an equivocal allegiance to the ideal of liberal education, which Newman identifies as "perfection of the intellect" consisting in this: "It is almost prophetic from its knowledge of history; it is almost heart-searching from its knowledge of human nature; it has almost supernatural charity from its freedom from littleness and prejudice; it has almost the repose of faith, because nothing can startle it; it has almost the beauty and harmony of heavenly contemplation, so intimate is it with the eternal order of things."[8]

But Newman sometimes incurred the suspicion, if not exactly the wrath, of authorities. In 1859, he published an essay called "On Consulting the Faithful in Matters of Doctrine", in which he argued the desirability of looking to the faith of faithful lay Catholics as helpful testimony to the authentic faith of the Church. The article fed suspicion of his orthodoxy in clerical circles in Britain and Rome. During the run-up to the First Vatican Council in 1870, he was among the "inopportunists" who believed the time was not ripe for a formal definition of papal infallibility. Nevertheless, he welcomed the formulation of the dogma adopted by the council and approved by Pope Pius IX and had no reservations thereafter about defending the doctrine vigorously.

No account of Newman would be complete without acknowledging that he was a man of considerable sensitivity who easily took offense. There were, for example, continuing tensions between him and the London Oratory over whether he, as founder of the Oratory in Britain, had a right to exercise authority over that house of the order. His

---

[8] John Henry Newman, *The Idea of a University* (Garden City, N.Y.: Doubleday Image Books, 1959), 160.

long relationship with Cardinal Henry Edward Manning of Westminster—like Newman, a former Anglican clergyman who converted to Catholicism—was often fraught.

But his skills as a controversialist came most fully and publicly into play in an extended conflict between him and Charles Kingsley, an Anglican clergyman and popular novelist who was conspicuously hostile to Catholicism. Kingsley had published a piece impugning the truthfulness of Catholic priests in general and Newman in particular. That led to a series of letters and public statements in which Newman demanded a retraction and Kingsley hedged. Most people following the affair concluded that Newman demolished Kingsley in debate. But years later, informed of Kingsley's death, Newman offered a Mass for him and said his old adversary had unintentionally become one of his "best friends" inasmuch as Kingsley's offensive remarks had prompted the writing of the work that forever secured his reputation—the *Apologia pro Vita Sua.*[9]

Published in 1865, the *Apologia* is a masterpiece of self-analysis and religious exposition. It is not, however, an easy book to read, especially since, in many cases, even reasonably well-educated people today have largely lost touch with the ideas and vocabulary of the religious tradition undergirding Western culture—a tradition that is, of course, fundamental to the story Newman has to tell. Nor is this an autobiography in the sense of the ghostwritten celebrity self-celebrations that often pass for autobiographies today, since Newman leaves out a great deal in providing exactly what he says he will—a "history of his religious opinions". But for those willing and able to rise to the effort required to follow the account of a deeply religious and scholarly man determined once and for all to explain what it is that

[9] Ker, *John Henry Newman*, 692.

he believes and why he believes it, his account is profoundly moving. The book begins with these words: "It may easily be conceived how great a trial it is to me to write the following history of myself; but I must not shrink from the task."[10] We can be glad he did not.

Other important works followed over the years, including the *Essay in Aid of a Grammar of Assent* (1870), a subtle, innovative study of the psychology and epistemology of religious faith, and the *Letter to the Duke of Norfolk* (1875), a spirited defense of the patriotism of British Catholics. Newman also published novels, poetry, historical studies, and several collections of his sermons.

In 1879, Pope Leo XIII named Newman a cardinal—an honor bestowed late in life but gladly received. As his cardinal's motto he chose a saying attributed to Saint Francis de Sales: *Cor ad cor loquitur* ("Heart speaks to heart"). In his later years, he lived quietly at the Birmingham Oratory while continuing to write and publish. He died there of pneumonia on August 11, 1890. On his memorial tablet were words he had chosen: *Ex umbris et imaginibus in veritatem* ("Out of shadows and things imagined into the truth"), a description of his religious journey perhaps but, even more so, of the passage to his eternal reward. He was declared a saint in 2019 by Pope Francis.

Saint John Henry Newman is regularly described as one of the most important theologians of modern times. His biographer Ian Ker speaks of him as "a Christian thinker who transcends his culture and his time, reminding one perhaps more of St. Augustine than of any other

[10] Newman, *Apologia*, 1.

comparable figure".[11] Catholic commentator George Weigel declares that long before Pope Saint John XXIII announced, in January 1959, his intention to call an ecumenical council, Newman had already identified "the crisis that such an assembly of Catholic leaders would have to address: the challenge of proclaiming the Gospel of Jesus Christ amid the civilizational crisis of a modernity that had cut itself loose from some of its deepest cultural roots".[12] Without pretending to give a complete answer to the question, it is appropriate here to sketch some of the ways in which Cardinal Newman did indeed lay out the "civilizational crisis of modernity" that Vatican II would need to address.

For much of his adult life, Newman's principal intellectual adversary was the phenomenon that he called "liberalism in religion". This should not be confused with "liberalism" in its secular political sense; as Newman used it, it refers to something quite different in the religious context. He provided a particularly clear explanation of it in the talk he gave in Rome on the occasion of being made a cardinal:

> Liberalism in religion is the doctrine that there is no positive truth in religion, but that one creed is as good as another, and this is the teaching which is gaining substance and force daily. It is inconsistent with any recognition of any religion, as *true*. It teaches that all are to be tolerated, for all are matters of opinion. Revealed religion is not a truth, but a sentiment and a taste; not an objective fact, not miraculous; and it is the right of each individual to make it say just what strikes his fancy. Devotion is not necessarily

founded on faith. Men may go to Protestant Churches and to Catholic, may get good from both and belong to neither. They may fraternize together in spiritual thoughts and feelings, without having any views at all of doctrines in common, or seeing the need of them. Since, then, religion is so personal a peculiarity and so private a possession, we must of necessity ignore it in the intercourse of man with man. If a man puts on a new religion every morning, what is that to you? It is as impertinent to think about as about his sources of income or his management of his family. Religion is in no sense the bond of society.[13]

This liberalism in religion, Newman told his listeners, was something he had resisted "for thirty, forty, fifty years", and now, more strongly than ever, he fought it as "an error overspreading, as a snare, the whole earth".[14]

Beyond liberalism, however, Newman saw rapidly spreading something even worse: atheism. This is how he speaks of it in the *Apologia*:

What a scene, what a prospect, does the whole of Europe present at this day! and not only Europe, but every government and every civilization through the world which is under the influence of the European mind! Especially ... how sorrowful in the view of religion, even taken in its most elementary, most attenuated form, is the spectacle presented to us by the educated intellect of England, France, and Germany!

Lovers of their country and of their race, religious men external to the Catholic Church have attempted various expedients to arrest fierce wilful human nature in its onward course and to bring it into subjection. The

[13] Quoted in Robert Royal, *A Deeper Vision: The Catholic Intellectual Tradition in the Twentieth Century* (San Francisco: Ignatius Press, 2015), 378.
[14] Ibid.

necessity of some form of religion for the interests of
humanity has been generally acknowledged: but where
was the concrete representative of things invisible which
would have the force and the toughness necessary to be a
breakwater against the deluge?[15]

Newman goes on to suggest that God in his generous providence has equipped the Catholic Church with
infallibility in order to "preserve religion in the world",[16]
but on the evidence since Newman wrote, one would
be hard put to make the case that this has turned the tide
so far. In any case, Pope John XXIII, in his famous 1962
opening speech to the ecumenical council, did not suggest anything like this. Rather, in words that Newman
would likely have applauded, he declared the "major
interest" of Vatican II to be "that the sacred heritage of
Christian truth be safeguarded and expounded with great
efficacy". And to that end, he said, "What is needed, and
what everyone imbued with a truly Christian, Catholic
and apostolic spirit craves today, is that this doctrine shall
be more widely known, more deeply understood, and
more penetrating in its effects on men's moral lives....
For this deposit of faith, or truths which are contained
in our time-honored teaching is one thing; the manner in
which these truths are set forth (with their meaning preserved intact) is something else."[17]

The ideas of John Henry Newman unquestionably
played an important role in shaping the Second Vatican
Council. This is true of his ideas on the development of

[15] Newman, *Apologia*, 221–22.

[16] Ibid., 223.

[17] The text of the pope's address is available on the website of Catholic
Culture (www.catholicculture.org) and many other places on the internet. It
also is available on the Vatican website, although not in an English translation.

doctrine as well as phenomena such as liberalism and atheism as significant factors shaping the world scene in which
the council took place. At the same time, however, Vatican II has often—and correctly—been criticized for taking
too bland an approach to these enemies of faith, in contrast
with Newman's tough-mindedness. It might have been
well for the Church if he had been even more of an influence there than he was.

Saint Thérèse of Lisieux

(January 2, 1873–September 30, 1897)

"I Ask Jesus to Draw Me into the Flames of His Love"

If all we knew about Saint Thérèse of Lisieux was that she wrote of herself as God's "little flower", we might suppose she was a hopeless sentimentalist. But read her classic *Story of a Soul*, and you will find that, despite the book's occasional lapses into the sentimental rhetoric typical of the late nineteenth century, its author was a strong, realistic young woman, wise beyond her years, with a will of iron where her vocation and the pursuit of sanctity were concerned. As one of her admirers points out, facing physical torment and a dark night of the spirit, "she remained determined to make her whole life, up until her last living breath, an act of love".[1]

But that was not always so. Sanctity was something she, just like other seekers after holiness, had to labor to achieve in the face of real difficulties.

Born on January 2, 1873, Marie-Francoise-Thérèse Martin was the youngest of nine children of Louis and Zélie Martin. She grew up in a loving, deeply Catholic, middle-class family in which four of her sisters became

---

[1] Stephanie Paulsell, "Reading St. Therese", *Harvard Divinity Bulletin* (Summer/Autumn 2010), https://bulletin.hds.harvard.edu/reading-st-therese/.

nuns—three Carmelites like her and one a Visitandine. But following her mother's death from breast cancer when Thérèse was four, she became a temperamental child prone to tantrums when things were not exactly as she wanted and ready to burst into tears with little or no provocation. "I really made a big fuss over everything", she later wrote.[2]

Then came her turning point. Following family tradition, after Midnight Mass on Christmas Eve 1886, Thérèse placed her empty shoes on the hearth to be filled with presents and candy and then headed upstairs with her sister Céline to put her hat away. Then they heard their frazzled father, thinking them out of earshot, say, "Fortunately, this will be the last year." Fearing her little sister would react to that with a crying fit, Céline told Thérèse not to go back down. And then, with no advance warning, a great change came over the younger girl. "I felt charity enter into my soul, and the need to forget myself and to please others." Rushing downstairs, she snatched up her shoes, took them to her father, and then joyfully opened her gifts while he looked on and laughed. She was a changed person from then on.[3]

Filled now with what she calls a "thirst for souls", Thérèse took up the cause of a man named Henri Pranzini, whom she had read about in the paper. Pranzini was a convicted murderer under sentence of death, and now Thérèse stormed heaven with prayers for him to repent. Nothing happened at first, but when the time came for him to die, a priest held out a crucifix to him, and Pranzini, who had shown no sign of remorse up to then, kissed Christ's wounds three times. Thérèse was certain he was

[2] Thérèse of Lisieux, *Story of a Soul*, trans. John Clarke, O.C.D., 3rd ed. (Washington, DC: ICS Publications, 1996), 91.
[3] Ibid., 135.

saved, and now the desire to go on saving souls became a permanent part of this formerly self-absorbed child's life.

Having watched eagerly as her older sisters entered the Carmelite convent in Lisieux, Thérèse longed to do the same. In November 1887, her father took her and Céline on a diocesan pilgrimage to Rome, and she boldly seized the opportunity of an audience with Pope Leo XIII to ask him to tell the authorities to let her enter Carmel even though she was underage. "You will enter if God wills it", the startled pontiff told the girl. Having hoped for more, Thérèse was crushed by that response, but soon the local bishop gave his approval, and on April 9, 1888, she entered Carmel at last.

Two years later, she made her profession of vows. She took the name Thérèse of the Child Jesus and the Holy Face. For the occasion, she wrote a make-believe wedding invitation reading in part, "Being unable to invite you to the Nuptial Blessing which was given on Mount Carmel, September 8, 1890 (the heavenly court alone was admitted), you are nevertheless asked to be present at the Return from the Wedding which will take place Tomorrow, the Day of Eternity, when Jesus, Son of God, will come on the Clouds of Heaven in the splendor of His Majesty, to judge the Living and the Dead. The hour being as yet uncertain, you are invited to hold yourselves in readiness and to watch."[4]

As those high-spirited words suggest, Thérèse was intensely happy. Soon, though, having unsurprisingly found that life in a strict convent was no bed of roses, she resolved to work on her interior life by using the opportunities that presented themselves to show affection and kindness to the least attractive of her sisters in religion. The story of Sister

[4] Ibid., 167–68.

St. Pierre, recounted in her autobiography, illustrates that.
Still a novice, Thérèse volunteered to accompany this elderly,
crotchety nun from choir to dinner every day while holding
tight to her helper's cincture to keep her steady. "But if by
mistake she took a false step", Thérèse wrote, "immediately
it appeared to her that I was holding her incorrectly and
she was about to fall. 'Ah! My God! You are going too fast;
I'm going to break something.' If I tried to go more slowly:
'Well, come on! Ah! I was right when I said you were too
young to help me.'" Reaching the refectory at last, Thérèse
helped the old nun get settled, turned up her sleeves—just
the way Sister wanted it done—and prepared to leave. Then
she saw that the old woman's arthritis made it hard for her
to cut her bread. So, without being asked, she cut Sister St.
Pierre's bread, "gave her my most beautiful smile", and left.
"It was by this means that I gained her entire good graces",
she adds.[5]

Taking a crotchety old nun to dinner was only one of
many opportunities afforded Thérèse for spiritual growth.
She tells of spending a cold winter night in the convent
infirmary, amid the shadows on dimly lighted brick walls,
where she was tending a sick nun. Suddenly she heard
in the distance lively music coming from a reception
where elegantly dressed partygoers were no doubt enjoy-
ing themselves, while her only company was a nun who
kept complaining about how poorly she felt. Suddenly she
received an illumination that filled her with joy. And if
she could be so happy now, she thought, "what will this
happiness be in heaven when one shall see ... the incom-
parable grace the Lord gave us when He chose us to dwell
in His house, heaven's real portal?"[6]

[5] Ibid., 247–48.
[6] Ibid., 248–49.

Through a multitude of small incidents like these, Thérèse perfected her famous "Little Way" to holiness. She was a small person with a small soul, she reasoned, and was living in a setting that invited only small deeds of kindness. But live that small life with great love in total obedience to God's will, and the result might be something great. "My vocation is love", she wrote.[7] To explain her meaning, she cited a recent invention of that day: "I wanted to find an elevator which would raise me to Jesus, for I am too small to climb the rough stairway to perfection."[8] And she told her prioress, "My dear Mother, you can see that I am a very little soul and that I can offer God only very little things."[9]

It was natural, too, that the Little Way should find expression in what she called spiritual childhood. Note that word "childhood": it is by no means the same as childishness. As applied to prayer and the interior life, which is how Thérèse applied it, it assumed a certain relationship, of child to parent, but one in which the child speaks out of love while supposing that the response of the parent, God, will not only proceed from reciprocal love but also be far beyond anything the child can imagine. Saint Thérèse gives this explanation:

> To be heard it is not necessary to read from a book some beautiful formula prepared for the occasion. If this were the case, alas, I would have to be pitied! Outside the Divine Office which I am very unworthy to recite, I do not have the courage to force myself to search out *beautiful* prayers in books.... I cannot recite them at all and not knowing which to choose, I do like children who do

[7] Ibid., 194.
[8] Ibid., 207.
[9] Ibid., 250.

not know how to read, I say very simply to God what I wish to say, without composing beautiful sentences, and He always understands me.[10]

Upon becoming assistant to the mistress of novices, Thérèse practiced the Little Way in that role, humble with some of the young women and "severe" with others, depending on what would be best for each. At the request of the prioress, she also became a spiritual sister to two French missionary priests, one in North Africa and the other in Indochina (Vietnam today), praying for them and sending them letters containing spiritual guidance and encouragement. And she composed poems and wrote a playlet about Joan of Arc, performed by the sisters.

On the night of Holy Thursday 1896, Thérèse coughed up blood. It signaled the presence of tuberculosis, an illness she welcomed in the belief that it would speed her journey to heaven. On July 8, 1897, she was transferred to the convent's infirmary. Her dying was a slow, painful process that was accompanied by temptations that sought to shake her faith in the reality of heaven. But the young woman who on Christmas Eve as a child of thirteen had suddenly seen her calling—to forget herself and concentrate on making others happy—now made this prediction: "I feel that my mission is about to begin, my mission of making others love God as I love Him, my mission of teaching my little way to souls. If God answers my requests, my heaven will be spent on earth up until the end of the world. Yes, I want to spend my heaven in doing good on earth."[11] She died on September 30.

Saint Thérèse of Lisieux was beatified by Pope Saint Pius X and was canonized on May 17, 1925, by Pope

---

[10] Ibid., 242.
[11] Ibid., 263.

Pius XI. "In spiritual childhood is the secret of sanctity for all the faithful", Pope Benedict XV said of her.[12] And when canonizing her, Pius XI declared that all the faithful are called to "enter wholeheartedly into the Little Way".[13] Declaring her to be "one of the great masters of the spiritual life in our time", Pope Saint John Paul II in 1997 formally recognized her as a Doctor (teacher) of the Church.[14] She is also recognized, with Saint Francis Xavier, the sixteenth-century Jesuit missionary to the Far East, as patroness of missions and missionaries, and, with Saint Joan of Arc, as secondary patroness of France. Her parents, Louis and Zélie Martin, were canonized by Pope Francis in 2015.

Speaking of her final illness and simultaneous spiritual affliction, Father John Clarke, O.C.D., translator of *Story of a Soul*, says of Saint Thérèse of Lisieux, "Her great trial of faith removes her forever from that category of sanctity in which she has been so often placed, the sweet sentimentality that none of us appreciates."[15] Here is an important point to grasp for anyone trying to understand this saint.

Stephanie Paulsell, a professor at the Harvard University Divinity School, tells how her own appreciation of Thérèse took shape over a period of years and three separate readings of her book. Upon first reading it at the age of twelve, she recalls, she loved the book and the picture

[12] Quoted in ibid., xii.

[13] Quoted in ibid., xii.

[14] John Paul II, apostolic letter *Divini Amoris Scientia* (October 19, 1997), no. 3.

[15] John Clarke, O.C.D., introduction to Thérèse of Lisieux, *Story of a Soul*, xviii.

of Thérèse that she took from it. But years later, when she was a graduate student, rereading it was a different story: "St. Therese had set my feet in a broad place when I was 12, but when I was 24, she herself seemed to me utterly hemmed in—trapped by her piety, by her times, by her culture, by her gender."

Years after came the third reading. And now Paulsell awoke to the fact that Thérèse spent the last year and a half of her life in what writers on mystical theology call "the dark night of the soul"—the terrifying sensation that God has turned his back and left one utterly without consolation. Facing the reality of her approaching death, Paulsell writes, Thérèse "fell into a trough of doubt and fear". And yet she persevered. "Even in this night of nothingness, even with her vision of God's love obscured, she stayed turned toward God, and she kept loving.... She never regained the joy of her faith and the consolations it had once provided. But she never stopped loving God either." Now, Paulsell concludes, her own view has changed: "St. Therese's 'little way' no longer seems so little.... Her little way invites us all to take the small steps that make the big steps possible."[16]

It is better, Saint Thérèse observes, to speak to God than about him. But attempting to practice the Little Way raises an unavoidable question: How is this particular speaking to be done? Certainly there are more ways than one. One way that comes to mind is more or less as equal to equal. Or, if that is not quite right, then in the manner in which a junior partner in a firm might address a senior partner: respectfully, that is, but with a full and unapologetic sense of entitlement to speak one's mind. Another is in the manner of a low-ranking servant speaking to a stern, not very

---

[16] Paulsell, "Reading St. Therese".

patient master: with frequent repetitions of "Excuse me" and "Pardon me for saying" and "Whatever seems best to you, sir." Too servile by half, I would say, although I do not hold that against anxious souls who fear to overstep some invisible line in addressing God.

In any case, the way of praying that Saint Thérèse proposes and practices is to speak to God as a child speaks to a loving and trusted Father. (But Thérèse notes candidly that in periods of marked aridity, when otherwise she had nothing to say in prayer, she simply repeated an Our Father and a Hail Mary—very slowly—and found as much nourishment in them as she would have had in repeating them over and over.)

However one might choose to pray, Saint Thérèse was a great believer in the practice. She writes,

> Was it not in prayer that St. Paul, St. Augustine, St. John of the Cross, St. Thomas Aquinas, St. Francis, St. Dominic, and so many other famous friends of God have drawn out this divine science which delights the greatest geniuses? A scholar has said: "*Give me a lever and a fulcrum and I will lift the world.*" What Archimedes was not able to obtain ... the saints have obtained in all its fullness. The Almighty has given them as *fulcrum: HIMSELF ALONE*; as lever: *PRAYER* which burns with a fire of love. And it is in this way that they have *lifted the world*; it is in this way that the saints still militant lift it, and that, until the end of time, the saints to come will lift it.[17]

Many people have come to Saint Thérèse over the years to learn her Little Way and have then commended it to others. Saint Josemaría Escrivá, the founder of Opus Dei, devotes two chapters to it in his popular book of

[17] Thérèse of Lisieux, *Story of a Soul*, 258.

meditations *The Way* and says this: "Spiritual childhood is not spiritual foolishness or softness; it is a sane and forceful way which, due to its difficult easiness, the soul must begin and then continue, led by the hand of God."[18]

The psychoanalyst and author Karl Stern quotes an imaginary skeptic dismissing spiritual childhood as "a poetic myth". Stern writes,

> It is true, children do hate, they do distrust and they are proud.... But we all have gone through an early phase of complete and utter dependence. We were helpless without our mother. We needed her in an all-out way.... That earliest Little Man, that Arche-Child of our ontogenetic story, is still alive in every one of us. To regress to it on the natural plane, in our relationship with people, is a most serious form of neurosis. To find our way back to it on the supernatural plane, in our relationship with God, is the highest degree of maturity.[19]

Regarding the experience of reading Thérèse, Stern also remarks that there are times when, putting aside clichés and gentler modes of expression, she speaks in language that is "daring", even "shocking". And then "suddenly you have something like an optical illusion—the 'sweet' and 'little' French girl disappears, and before you stands an immense, awe-inspiring timeless figure, a companion of the Prophets, the Apostles, the Fathers of the Church and of the great mystics of the Middle Ages."[20]

The extraordinary words addressed to her prioress with which *Story of a Soul* closes have something of that quality:

---

[18] Josemaría Escrivá, *The Way*, no. 855 (New York: Scepter Publishers, 1982), 295–96.

[19] Karl Stern, "St. Therese of Lisieux", in *Saints for Now*, ed. Clare Boothe Luce (New York: Sheed and Ward, 1952), 308.

[20] Ibid., 302.

Dear Mother, this is my prayer. I ask Jesus to draw me into the flames of His love, to unite me so closely to Him that He live and act in me. I feel that the more the fire of love burns within my heart, the more I shall say: *"Draw me,"* the more also the souls who will approach me … *will run swiftly in the odor of the ointments of their Beloved*, for a soul that is burning with love cannot remain inactive.…

Since Jesus has reascended into heaven, I can follow Him only in the traces He has left, but how luminous these traces are! how perfumed! I have only to cast a glance in the Gospels and immediately I breathe in the perfumes of Jesus' life, and I know on which side to run. I don't hasten to the first place but to the last; rather than advance like the Pharisee, I repeat, filled with confidence, the publican's humble prayer. Most of all I imitate the conduct of Magdalene; her astonishing or rather her loving audacity which charms the Heart of Jesus also attracts my own. Yes, I feel it; even though I had on my conscience all the sins that can be committed, I would go, my heart broken with sorrow, and throw myself into Jesus' arms, for I know how much He loves the prodigal child who returns to Him. It is not because God, in his anticipating Mercy, has preserved my soul from mortal sin that I go to Him with confidence and love.[21]

And there she stopped and could write no more.

---

[21] Thérèse of Lisieux, *Story of a Soul*, 258–59.

Pope Saint Paul VI

(September 26, 1897–August 6, 1978)

"Am I Hamlet or Don Quixote?"

In the right—or should I say wrong?—circumstances, most of us can have a hard time doing the right thing, but it is doubly difficult for highly conscientious souls who truly want to do what is right but are not sure what it is. That is how it was with Pope Saint Paul VI, who wrote of himself, "Am I Hamlet or Don Quixote?" For a long time, conflicting strands of his personality, represented by the Danish prince who was tortured by uncertainty and the idealistic old knight who tilted at windmills, appeared to tug at Pope Paul while he wrestled with the question of contraception.

If, as one hopes, there is a special reward in heaven for sensitive people who do their duty in the face of obstacles, including those arising from their own hesitancy in saying for sure what duty requires in some difficult case, then Paul VI's reward must be great indeed. For at the turning point in his pontificate, this pope not only agonized over deciding where duty lay but also found himself having to pay dearly for having acted on his convictions.

In a general way, he may have seen it coming. Only six weeks after becoming pope, he wrote privately, "I was solitary before, but now my solitariness becomes complete and awesome.... My duty is to plan, decide, assume every responsibility for guiding others, even when it seems illogical and perhaps absurd. And to suffer alone—me and God." By the end, comments historian Eamon Duffy, "tribulation had become the element he moved in."[1]

Bearing the weight of the papacy in troubled times that included not only the personal abuse hurled at him over the contraception issue but also a tidal wave of defections by priests and nuns and open dissent extending to many Church doctrines besides the teaching on birth control— and all this amid a cultural revolution that shook the Catholic Church along with other pillars of social stability—Paul was moved to write, "I am full of consolation, overcome with joy, throughout every tribulation."[2] Reading that, one recalls words of another man named Paul: "As we share abundantly in Christ's sufferings, so through Christ we share abundantly in comfort too" (2 Cor 1:5).

Giovanni Battista Montini was born on September 26, 1897, in Concesio, a village in northern Italy near Brescia. People who take note of such things will find significance in the fact that this was only four days before the death of Saint Thérèse of Lisieux, an exemplary figure of nineteenth-century Catholicism, just as Montini was to be in the Church of the twentieth century. His father, Giorgio, was a lawyer, journalist, Catholic Action leader, and member of the Italian Parliament. The shy, bookish young man entered the seminary in 1916 and was ordained a priest in 1920. In Rome, he studied at the Gregorian University, Sapienza University, and the Pontifical Ecclesiastical Academy, the training school where selected priests prepare for careers as Vatican diplomats and officials of the Secretariat of State.

---

[1] Eamon Duffy, *Saints and Sinners: A History of the Popes* (New Haven, Conn.: Yale University Press, 2006), 367.
[2] Ibid.

Following a brief stint at the Holy See's embassy in Poland that was cut short by illness, he returned to Rome and began work in the Secretariat of State, where he was to remain until 1954. In 1937, with Cardinal Eugenio Pacelli now secretary of state, Monsignor Montini was named *sostituto* for ordinary affairs—in effect, assistant secretary of state—the position he continued to occupy after Cardinal Pacelli, on the eve of World War II in 1939, was elected pope. In effect, Montini was now Pope Pius XII's chief of staff and right-hand man.

During the war, he directed the information office set up within the Secretariat of State to handle requests from family members and others seeking to locate refugees, deportees, and prisoners of war. Between 1941 and 1944, the office received requests from more than 102,000 Jewish sources alone and was able to provide information to roughly a third.

Montini also channeled directives from Pius XII to Vatican diplomats throughout Europe, instructing them on steps to take to assist Jews fleeing the Nazis. During the German occupation of Rome in 1943, he carried out the pope's directive to "do everything possible" to find shelter for the city's Jews, then facing deportation to death camps. As a result of these efforts, many found refuge in convents, monasteries, and other religious houses, including the Vatican and the papal residence outside the city at Castel Gandolfo. These efforts alone are credited with saving more than eight thousand Jews.[3]

Monsignor Montini deeply admired Pope Pius XII. But in 1954, Pius named him to head the Archdiocese of Milan, a move commonly attributed to a falling-out between Pius and Montini due to Montini's relatively liberal views. That

---

[3] Michael Hesemann, *The Pope and the Holocaust* (San Francisco: Ignatius Press, 2022), 354–81 passim.

may be. But it seems equally possible that the pope sent him to the huge northern archdiocese—1,000 churches, 2,500 priests, 3.5 million Catholics—with an eye to giving him experience in managing a major see in the expectation that he might one day become pope.

In 1958, the new pope, John XXIII, named Montini a cardinal. A month later, Pope John announced his intention to convene an ecumenical council bringing together the bishops of the Church from all over the world.

Cardinal Montini's initial skepticism regarding this project has often been quoted: "This holy old boy [John XXIII] doesn't know what a hornet's nest he's stirring up." Once the council began, however, Montini emerged as a major figure at its crucial first session in the fall of 1962. The following summer, Pope John died, and Cardinal Montini was elected to succeed him, taking the name Paul VI. Among his first acts was to announce that he would continue Vatican II. He presided over three more sessions, brought the assembly to a successful conclusion in 1965, and set about working for its implementation.

The early years of his pontificate brought dazzling successes on several fronts. Along with implementing Vatican II, these included a historic meeting in Jerusalem with the Orthodox Church's ecumenical patriarch of Constantinople and subsequent steps toward healing the millennium-old split between Catholicism and Orthodoxy; a much-applauded 1965 visit to the United Nations General Assembly in New York, where Paul VI electrified listeners with a dramatic appeal for "No more war"; and publication in 1967 of an important social encyclical called *Populorum Progressio* (On the Development of Peoples), which aligned the Church with the concerns of the world's developing nations. The encyclical pointed to a threefold duty of wealthy countries: mutual solidarity ("the aid that the richer nations must give to developing nations"), social justice ("the rectification of trade relations between strong and weak nations"), and universal charity ("the effort to build a more humane world community, where all can give and receive, and where the progress of some is not bought at the expense of others").[4]

Things seemed to be going swimmingly for Pope Paul. Then came birth control.

Shortly before his death, Pope John XXIII had established a Commission on Population, Family, and Birth Rate to prepare for the Holy See's participation in a coming population conference sponsored by the United Nations and the World Health Organization. Appointed secretary-general of the commission was Father Henri de Riedmatten, O.P., an official of the Secretariat of State. In short order, responding to requests, Pope Paul expanded the group's mandate to include the Church's teaching on contraception, and soon it was universally known as the "birth control commission".

Among those associated with the commission, first as a member and then, after membership was limited to the hierarchy, as a theological adviser, was Father John C. Ford, S.J., a prominent moral theologian from the United States. As work progressed, Father Ford invited the assistance of Professor Germain Grisez, a young American philosopher teaching at Georgetown University who had lately published a carefully reasoned defense of the Church's traditional teaching on contraception. Years later, Grisez posted on his website, the Way of the Lord Jesus, a biographical sketch of Father Ford with an insider account of the maneuvering that accompanied the commission's work.[5]

[4] Paul VI, encyclical letter *Populorum Progressio* (March 26, 1967), no. 44.
[5] See Germain Grisez, The Way of the Lord Jesus, http://www.twotlj.org.

According to Grisez, Pope Paul had been persuaded that the new oral contraceptive—the Pill—"might not be contraception" in conflict with the Church's teaching, and he therefore wanted a "thorough study ... to ensure that the Church would not ask more of faithful Catholic married couples than God did".[6] Several years of intense debate and politicking followed within the commission, with a majority eventually supporting contraception.

Plans were laid to publicize this conclusion, but the pope, evidently aware of what was in the works, told a conference in Rome on October 29, 1966, that the commission could not decide the question inasmuch as it involved "doctrinal, pastoral and social" issues beyond its competence. The scheme to publicize the birth control commission's views as if they settled the matter then collapsed. But six months later, internal commission documents—inaccurately labeled "majority" and "minority" reports—were leaked with the obvious intention of putting pressure on the pope.

And so, finally, in late July 1968, Pope Paul published his encyclical *Humanae Vitae*. Declaring it the "constant doctrine" of the Church that "each and every marital act must of necessity retain its intrinsic relationship to the procreation of human life", the pope cautioned that "to use this divine gift while depriving it, even if only partially, of its meaning and purpose, is equally repugnant to the nature of man and of woman, and is consequently in opposition to the plan of God and His holy will."[7]

The encyclical has been praised as a prophetic document anticipating what would happen as a result of the widespread acceptance of contraception, then already well

[6] Germain Grisez, in a personal conversation with the author.
[7] Paul VI, encyclical *Humanae Vitae* (July 25, 1968), nos. 11, 13.

underway, including "marital infidelity and a general lowering of moral standards".[8] But the immediate reaction was noisy dissent, some spontaneous but some clearly orchestrated—for example, a full-page ad rejecting the doctrine and carrying the signatures of scores of clerics that appeared in the *New York Times* just a day after the encyclical had been issued.[9]

In some ways, *Humanae Vitae* could not have come at a worse time—at the height of a cultural revolution, in large part a revolution in sexual morality, sweeping the Western world. In the United States and other countries, large numbers of priests and religious were abandoning the priesthood and religious life, and new vocations were plummeting. Mass attendance had begun a decline that continued well into the next century, with no end in sight as this is written. Ordinary Catholics were scandalized and confused. Matters reached such a point that, in a homily on June 29, 1972, Pope Paul declared that "the smoke of Satan has entered the temple of God."[10]

And yet these troubled years did bring some papal bright spots amid the encircling gloom. One was the publication in December 1975 of Paul VI's document on evangelization, *Evangelii Nuntiandi*. Its message, both sophisticated and inspirational, set the stage for a fresh emphasis on

[8] Ibid., no. 17.

[9] Catholic writer Robert Royal remarks that the technique of organized dissent via media so visible in this episode soon became entrenched, to such an extent that when, in 1990, the Vatican published a document suggesting that dissenting theologians would do well to pursue the "slower and quieter path of dialogue", it was met with "angry outrage". Robert Royal, *A Deeper Vision: The Catholic Intellectual Tradition in the Twentieth Century* (San Francisco: Ignatius Press, 2015), 125.

[10] Quoted in William Doino Jr., "The Smoke of Satan Returns", *First Things*, October 28, 2013, https://www.firstthings.com/web-exclusives/2013/10/the -smoke-of-satan-returns.

spreading the gospel among "the people of today", whom it described as "buoyed up by hope but at the same time oppressed by fear and distress".[11] That the revival of evangelization urged by Paul VI remains very far from being taken up among well-to-do Catholics in wealthy nations is hardly his fault.

Unquestionably, though, Pope Paul's last years were a time of sadness, even tragedy, epitomized by the kidnapping and brutal murder by left-wing terrorists of his old friend Aldo Moro, leader of Italy's Christian Democratic Party. The pope pleaded publicly for Moro's release but to no avail. The terrorists killed him, and Paul, in his last public act, presided at his friend's funeral. A few days later, while resting at Castel Gandolfo, he suffered a massive heart attack and died on August 6, 1978. He was canonized by Pope Francis on October 14, 2018.

When Paul VI asked that famous question, "Am I Hamlet or Don Quixote?" he was acknowledging that the tension between painful uncertainties and unfashionable ideals was part of his makeup. But there was more than that to Pope Saint Paul. His legacy is in the concluding passage of *Humanae Vitae*, the encyclical that was his turning point.

After speaking there of "the work of education, of progress and of charity" that lay ahead for him and others, he adds this: "We are convinced that this truly great work will bring blessings both on the world and on the Church. For man cannot attain that true happiness for which he yearns with all the strength of his spirit, unless he keeps the laws which the Most High God has engraved in his very nature. These laws must be wisely and lovingly

[11] Paul VI, apostolic exhortation *Evangelii Nuntiandi* (December 8, 1975), no. 1.

observed."[12] Progress, wisdom, love—a good program for
a pope, come to think of it.

It is impossible to isolate a particular moment in the long,
complex process preceding *Humanae Vitae* as the precise
point at which Pope Paul decided that he should con-
firm the Church's condemnation of artificial birth control
by affirming "the inseparable connection, established by
God" between the "unitive" and "procreative" (sometimes
expressed simply as love-giving and life-giving) meanings
of the conjugal act.[13] Indeed, his lengthy deliberative process itself appears to have been a kind of extended turning
point during which he became increasingly aware that,
although approving contraception might make him briefly
popular, for him to do otherwise than he eventually did
would have disastrous consequences for the Church and
the world.

After declaring that adding the Catholic Church's voice
to the chorus of approval for contraception would further broaden the already "wide and easy" road to "marital infidelity and a general lowering of moral standards",
Paul then shifts the focus beyond individual behavior to
the level of public policy: the "danger of this power passing into the hands of those public authorities who care
little for the precepts of the moral law" and who would
then likely turn to forced contraception as an instrument
of population limitation.[14] With the advantage of hind-
sight, we now see how the contraceptive mentality drives

[12] Paul VI, *Humanae Vitae*, no. 31.
[13] Ibid., no. 12.
[14] Ibid., no. 17.

the legalization of abortion and—embarrassing irony—has
helped bring about the unintended consequence of radical
population shrinkage now taking place in nations around
the globe.[15]

Pope Paul's vision was not confined to the social ills
flowing from contraception. His 1975 apostolic exhortation *Evangelii Nuntiandi* is relevant here for its analysis of
the obstacles to evangelization. Declaring secularism the
most striking feature of modern times, Pope Paul points
to new forms of atheism—"pragmatic, systematic and
militant"—arising from it.[16] Moreover, side by side with
the atheism inspired by secularism is the large number of
baptized but nonpracticing people. And the members of all
these groups are resistant to evangelization:

> The resistance of [atheists and nonbelievers] takes the form
> of a certain refusal and an inability to grasp the new order of
> things, the new meaning of the world, of life and of his
> tory; such is not possible if one does not start from a divine
> absolute. The resistance of the [baptized but nonpracticing]
> takes the form of inertia and the slightly hostile attitude of
> the person ... who claims to know it all and to have tried it
> all and who no longer believes it.[17]

In this context, then, the pope turns to evangelization
and the fact that its impact is weakened where those who
profess their allegiance to the gospel are divided among

---

[15] As this is written, world population is projected to stop growing before
the present century ends. Particularly striking current examples are Japan and
China. A fertility rate of 2.1 children per woman is necessary to maintain population at a stable level. According to www.macrotrends.net, the fertility rate
in China in 2023 was 1.705, in Japan 1.367, and in Europe 1.615. At present,
U.S. population continues to increase due to immigration, but as of 2023, the
fertility rate was 1.784.

[16] Paul VI, *Evangelii Nuntiandi*, no. 55.

[17] Ibid., no. 56.

themselves. And he asks, "Is this not perhaps one of the great sicknesses of evangelization today? Indeed, if the Gospel that we proclaim is seen to be rent by doctrinal disputes, ideological polarizations or mutual condemnations among Christians ... how can those to whom we address our preaching fail to be disturbed, disoriented, even scandalized?"[18]

Nevertheless, *Evangelii Nuntiandi* ends with a positive challenge: "As evangelizers, we must offer Christ's faithful not the image of people divided and separated by unedifying quarrels, but the image of people who are mature in faith and capable of finding a meeting-point beyond the real tensions, thanks to a shared, sincere and disinterested search for truth. Yes, the destiny of evangelization is certainly bound up with the witness of unity given by the Church. This is a source of responsibility and also of comfort."[19]

Less than three years later, Paul VI was succeeded by Pope John Paul I and, after that pontificate was cut short by the new pope's death after only thirty-three days in office, by Cardinal Karol Wojtyła, who took the name John Paul II. In his first encyclical, *Redemptor Hominis* (The Redeemer of Man), John Paul II predictably paid tribute to his two immediate predecessors, but what he said about Pope Paul VI was more than routine politeness. That was particularly true when it came to "critical attitudes" said to have attacked the Church *ab intra*—from within—during Paul's pontificate.

John Paul conceded that this criticism had "various causes" and was "not always without sincere love for the Church". But then the new pope struck a tougher note:

[18] Ibid., no. 77.
[19] Ibid.

"Nevertheless criticism too should have its just limits. Otherwise it ceases to be constructive ... but [expresses] a wish to direct the opinion of others in accordance with one's own, which is at times spread abroad in too thoughtless a manner." And his predecessor as pope? "Gratitude is due to Paul VI because, while respecting every particle of truth contained in the various human opinions, he preserved at the same time the providential balance of the bark's helmsman."[20] Sounding rather like a new captain taking command of an old ship whose previous skipper had brought her safely through especially rough seas, John Paul II went on to say that, thanks to Paul VI, the Church as he found it was "more resistant with respect to the various 'novelties', more mature in her spirit of discerning, better able to bring out of her everlasting treasure 'what is new and what is old' [Mt 13:52] ... and because of all that more serviceable for her mission of salvation for all".[21]

[20] John Paul II, encyclical letter *Redemptor Hominis* (March 4, 1979), no. 4.
[21] Ibid.

Dorothy Day

(November 9, 1897–November 29, 1980)

"The Only Solution Is Love and Love Comes with Community"

Dorothy Day famously said she hoped the Church would never declare her a saint since, if that happened, people would stop paying attention to what she said. Whether Day gets her wish—and as this is written, the process that could bring formal recognition of her sainthood is in the Vatican's hands—veneration of this radical champion of social justice, pacifism, and Catholic doctrine remains strong. So strong, indeed, that in 2023 it reached the point (admittedly short of canonization) of giving a new Staten Island ferryboat her name.

Above all, say the authors of a Day biography, she not only asked hard questions but also answered them for herself and then did her best to live accordingly. Of course, they add, Day's answers and way of life "offer little to please the skeptical, the covetous, and the complacent".[1]

She was born on November 8, 1897, in Brooklyn Heights and baptized in an Episcopalian church, after which her parents exhibited no interest in her religious upbringing. From an early age, nonetheless, she manifested

---

[1] John Loughery and Blythe Randolph, *Dorothy Day: Dissenting Voice of the American Century* (New York: Simon and Schuster, 2020), 6.

a spontaneous receptivity to things of the spirit. Having learned a bit about praying from a Catholic neighbor, she began inventing long prayers of her own while she and her younger sister, Della, played at being saints. "It was a game with us", she explains in her autobiography, *The Long Loneliness.*[2]

Her father was a newspaperman whose work took the family from New York to San Francisco and from there to Chicago. In Chicago, Day, a teenager by now, began to read such writers as Upton Sinclair and Jack London, whose fictionalized jeremiads against social injustices stimulated her emerging social conscience. As early as age fifteen, she writes, she was convinced that "God meant man to be happy.... We did not need to have quite so much destitution and misery as I saw all around."[3] With a three-hundred-dollar scholarship earned in a competitive examination, she enrolled at the University of Illinois, joined the Socialist Party, continued to read radical writers, and nurtured her growing scorn for churchgoers uninterested in making a better world.

Leaving the university after two years, Day moved alone to New York and there began a journalistic career writing for socialist papers. From the start, her writing displayed a keen eye for the physical trappings of poverty, along with powerful empathy with the poor, as in the following passage from a November 13, 1916, article in the *New York Call*—the first front-page piece to carry her byline:

> Mrs. Salvatore is a little Italian woman who lives down in the Sheepshead Bay region; she has a face of uneven prettiness, and a brave little smile that contradicts the struggling

---

[2] Dorothy Day, *The Long Loneliness* (Garden City, N.Y.: Doubleday Image Books, 1959), 23.
[3] Ibid., 37.

expression in her eyes. She said, with the queer smile, that the cost of living did not bother her at all. "You just have to hunt a little longer for cheap stores, and think a little longer for different ways of serving unappetizing, or so-called unappetizing, messes. It's fun." But all the while there was that little crucified smile....

"Last year," she went on, "we used to buy liver and chicken feet for the dog. Pretty soon we took to eating the liver ourselves. Then, one time when my husband and I were out of work, and we had nothing else in the house to eat but some chicken feet that were to be cooked up for the puppy I thought of cooking them up for the family. You know, we have six.... So I peeled them all, cut off the nails and boiled them for a long time; of course it was a long time, but when it was done there was a thick jelly that we could eat on our bread."[4]

Sometimes Day wrote about pickets, and sometimes she joined them. In 1917, she took part in a women's suffrage demonstration outside the White House, was arrested along with other demonstrators, and served time in jail, where she read the Bible and was deeply moved by the psalms. This was the first of what would be a long series of arrests and jailings for joining demonstrations in support of causes from securing votes for women to opposing nuclear testing.

Although Day may someday be declared a saint, her life before her conversion was not saintly. She hobnobbed with journalists, writers, intellectuals, and especially men and women of the Left—anarchists, socialists, communists—and lived a bohemian lifestyle with the playwright Eugene O'Neill and others, according to her notion of how a liberated woman lived. In 1919, she had an abortion in

[4] "Mr. J.D. Rockefeller, 26 Broadway: Here's a Family Living on Dog Food", in Tom McDonough, *An Eye for Others: Dorothy Day, Journalist 1916–1917* (Washington, D.C.: Clemency Press, n.d.), 38.

Chicago—a harrowing experience that left her fearful of being unable to bear children.

For a time, she prepared to be a nurse, attending early Sunday Mass in the hospital chapel with one of her colleagues, but after a year, she gave up nursing in favor of writing. She wrote a semi-autobiographical novel, *The Eleventh Virgin*, and, with money from a movie studio for film rights, bought a little beach house on Staten Island. At that time, she and a man named Forster Batterham entered into what she called a common-law marriage.

By then, Day had begun praying regularly and sometimes attending Mass. Much to her joy, she became pregnant and, in March 1926, gave birth to a daughter, whom she named Tamar Teresa, in honor of Saint Teresa of Avila. She was determined to have her child baptized, but Forster was dead set against the idea, and Dorothy hesitated. One day, as she walked to the village for groceries, saying the Rosary as she went, she encountered an elderly nun named Sister Aloysia. The two became friendly, and Sister Aloysia agreed to arrange for Tamar's baptism. She also chided Day: "How can your daughter be brought up a Catholic unless you become one yourself?"

That was a question she was ready to hear. Day writes, "My very experience as a radical, my whole make-up, led me to want to associate myself with others, with the masses, in loving and praising God. Without even looking into the claims of the Catholic Church, I was willing to admit that for me she was the one true Church."[5] The nun drilled her in the catechism, and in July 1927, Tamar was baptized. In December, with Sister Aloysia as godmother, Day was conditionally baptized and made her first confession and Communion. The final break with Forster predictably followed.

[5] Day, *The Long Loneliness*, 135.

So now she was a Catholic, though hardly a conventional one. "I loved the Church", she says, but she also judged the Church to be in league with "the forces of reaction" that she, a leftist radical, regarded with disgust.[6] And now she faced another question: What could she possibly do to bring her faith and her social commitment together? Day's turning point was at hand without her knowing it.

At this time, the Great Depression had settled over America. After covering a communist-organized hunger march on Washington for the Catholic magazine *Commonweal*, she knelt in prayer in the nation's capital in the shadowy crypt church of the Shrine of the Immaculate Conception. The date was December 8, 1932, the feast of the Immaculate Conception of Mary, the mother of Christ. "I offered up a special prayer," Day writes, "a prayer which came with tears and with anguish, that some way would open up for me to use what talents I possessed for my fellow workers, for the poor."[7] Returning to New York, she found waiting for her (at the suggestion of a mutual friend) "a short, stocky man in his mid-fifties, as ragged and rugged as any of the marchers I had left"— Peter Maurin. Neither knew it, but the Catholic Worker had just been born.

Maurin, it turned out, was a French peasant and self-taught social theorist with an idea for a reform movement that would combine radical communitarianism with intense religious faith. As he presented it, what he envisaged was no less than a top-to-bottom reorganization of society—a peaceful revolution—that would create a world in which all men and women could live good, fulfilling lives. Says Day, "I can well recognize the fact that people remaining as they are, Peter's program is impossible. But it

[6] Ibid., 145.
[7] Ibid., 161.

would become actual, given a people changed in heart and mind, so that they would observe the new commandment of love, or desire to."[8]

With Maurin as her inspiration and guide, Day set out to make that happen.

Maurin died in 1949, but by then, thanks largely to Day's energy and vision, the Catholic Worker was a significant presence in American Catholicism and, to some extent, in the larger society, not only helping the poor and the outcast but also offering a rallying point for activists and idealists. Its projects included the *Catholic Worker* newspaper, which began publication in 1933 and sold for one cent per copy; its houses of hospitality, refuges for the needy and the homeless, of which Day writes, "The surroundings may be harsh; but where love is, God is";[9] and Catholic Worker farms established in pursuit of the movement's back-to-the-land philosophy.

Day never sacrificed her sometimes unpopular principles for the sake of popularity. She was resolutely faithful in her commitment to the doctrine of the Catholic Church, including the condemnation of birth control. She refused to repudiate the communists who had been her friends. She was unyieldingly committed to pacifism and nonviolence and opposed U.S. entry into World War II—a stance not universally welcomed by her fellow Catholic Workers. She condemned the dropping of atomic bombs on Hiroshima and Nagasaki. A frequent participant in peace demonstrations, she was arrested several times for refusing to participate in nuclear air-raid drills and in 1956 had the hellish experience of spending thirty days in the women's house of detention on Rikers Island in New York.

---

[8] Ibid., 167.
[9] Dorothy Day, *Loaves and Fishes: The Inspiring Story of the Catholic Worker Movement* (New York: Harper and Row, 1963), 215.

Dorothy Day died of a heart attack on November 29, 1980. Forty years later, there were reportedly more than 150 Catholic Worker houses and farms across the United States and elsewhere. Author Larry Chapp, a former theology professor who heads a Catholic Worker farm near Wilkes-Barre, Pennsylvania, says that in recent times the movement has "departed from [Day's] deeply Catholic vision and has embraced modern leftist social ideology instead", thereby calling into question its future "precisely as a Catholic enterprise". But Chapp also sees "pockets of hope" in the movement, citing several unnamed young Catholic Workers engaged in "starting Worker houses and farms which seek to adhere to the Catholic vision of Day and Maurin".[10]

Day is buried in Resurrection Cemetery on Staten Island. The headstone on her grave reads simply, "Dorothy Day, November 8, 1897—November 29, 1980/Deo Gratias". But her granddaughter Kate Hennessy finds rather more to say:

> Dorothy's life, her work and words, can be utterly uncomfortable. Pick any element of the Catholic Worker program and philosophy, and you might find yourself running for the hills. Opening houses of hospitality in which nothing is asked of those who are given refuge, whether the "deserving" or "undeserving" poor. Her stance on nonviolence can provoke people into anger, and her insistence on voluntary poverty cuts at the very roots of our society and most of what we strive for.... There are no bromides to be found here, no cheap grace, no sentimentality, no soothing or sensible solutions. And yet, paradoxically, all

---

[10] Larry Chapp, "Wither the Catholic Worker Movement?", *National Catholic Register*, April 6, 2023, https://www.ncregister.com/commentaries /whither-the-catholic-worker-movement.

of these Catholic Worker elements also have such capacity
to lead to joy.[11]

Besides those who accepted poverty as part of the rule of
their religious orders—Saint Teresa, Saint Thérèse, Saint
Ignatius Loyola—the profiles in this book include two laypeople who lived two very different versions of voluntary
poverty: Saint Benedict Joseph Labre and Dorothy Day.

In his classic *The Varieties of Religious Experience*, William
James cites Benedict Joseph Labre as an embodiment of an
"ever-recurring note" in accounts of holy people: They
place themselves entirely in God's hands, hold nothing
back, leave it to the Lord to provide what they need, and
deal with whatever wealth and possessions come their way
by selling them and giving the proceeds to the poor. This is
how they seek a higher sort of security.[12] G. K. Chesterton,
writing of Francis of Assisi, sees poverty lived this way as a
key to freedom from external coercion. It is a waste of time,
he says, to threaten a man who is eager to fast with cutting
back on his meals, or to wave the specter of impoverish-
ment in the face of a man who already lives by begging.[13]

Dorothy Day practiced voluntary poverty partly as
ascetical self-discipline and partly as a way to identify with
the poor whose *involuntary* poverty was forced on them by
external circumstances or, in not a few cases, by their own
weakness acting in concert with an inhuman economic

[11] Kate Hennessy, "A Revolution of the Heart: Learning from Dorothy
Day", *Tablet* (London), June 10, 2023.

[12] William James, *The Varieties of Religious Experience* (London: Longmans,
Green, 1929), 321.

[13] *Saint Francis of Assisi*, in *The Collected Works of G. K. Chesterton*, vol. 2 (San
Francisco: Ignatius Press, 1986), 94.

system. Her living of poverty was an ongoing catechesis of protest against that system as well as a way of realizing her vision of social justice. And part of poverty as she lived it lay in tending to the frequently annoying—and repeated—tasks of running an institution to house and feed the involuntary poor.

She writes,

> In the New York house, we buy a great deal of coffee, sugar, milk, tea, and oleo. Our butcher is a friend who gives us meat at a very cheap price. We get free fish from the market—the tails and heads from swordfish after the steaks have been cut off.... But our problem is not just one of food. For the rents we must have cash. This comes to more than a thousand dollars a month, not to speak of taxes on the Staten Island farm, which are now fifteen hundred a year and going up all the time. Gas and electric for a dozen apartments, as well as the houses of hospitality, are especially heavy in winter....
>
> Somehow the dollars that come in cover current bills, help us to catch up with payments on back debts, and make it possible for us to keep on going.[14]

But Day's poverty meant more than just scrambling to pay bills. Her biographers see in it a "Jansenist aspect", illustrated in her habit of staying at the "cheapest, most spartan" hotels she could find when she traveled. But Jansenism aside, they are quick to add, much more often her poverty was "simply the means by which she, and those who chose to follow her example, could feel the living presence of Jesus in their daily lives and more fruitfully obey his commands".[15]

[14] Day, *Loaves and Fishes*, 86–87.
[15] Loughery and Randolph, *Dorothy Day*, 317–18.

When not on the road giving talks and meeting with
the people of local Worker groups, Day usually lived at the
house of hospitality in Manhattan. She gives this lively
account of life there:

> The Rosary said, we settle down for a few hours' work
> before the dinner crowd begins to come in. It will be
> more noisy and undisciplined than the noon crowd from
> the Bowery, including as it does all the staff and their
> friends, many of the latter being members of other peace
> groups who use our place to store their signs and get a hot
> meal. Whenever there is a specially fragrant dish cook-
> ing, such as pork chops or Italian sausage, the tantalizing
> odor spreads far and wide. The news seems to travel by
> grapevine. Then sometimes more people turn up than we
> have chops or sausage for, and we have recourse to soup
> again. Which means everybody crowds onto the first floor
> at once, hoping to secure the next place at table. "Always
> room for one more."
>
> How many times, all through my life, have I surveyed
> these tables and wondered if the bread would go around....
> Where does it all go? Where do all the people come from?
> How will it all be paid for? But the miracle is that it does
> get paid for, sooner or later. The miracle is, also, that sel-
> dom do more people come in than we can feed.[16]

Few of us are called to the literal practice of voluntary
poverty as part of our personal vocations. Does that let
us off the hook? By no means. The *Catechism of the Catholic Church* says, "Detachment from riches is obligatory
for entrance into the Kingdom of heaven", and it adds,
"Desire for true happiness frees man from his immoder-
ate attachment to the goods of this world so that he can

[16] Day, *Loaves and Fishes*, 212–13.

find his fulfillment in the vision and beatitude of God."[17]
Dorothy Day would have liked that, as these words of
hers suggest: "The greatest challenge of the day is: how to
bring about a revolution of the heart, a revolution which
has to start with each one of us? When we begin to take
the lowest place, to wash the feet of others, to love our
brothers with that burning love, that passion, which led to
the Cross, then we can truly say, 'Now I have begun.'"[18]

---

[17] *Catechism of the Catholic Church*, nos. 2544, 2548 (hereafter cited as *CCC*).
[18] Day, *Loaves and Fishes*, 210.

C. S. Lewis

(November 29, 1898–November 22, 1963)

"A Great Campaign of Sabotage"

Tracing the spiritual journey of C. S. Lewis requires quite a bit more than simply noting the one final point at which he declared himself a Christian. When that happened is, after all, clear enough from his own account. But mapping a series of events that stretched over several decades and led up to it could well have been a different matter. Fortunately, however, like Saint Augustine writing his *Confessions*, Lewis, too, provided a carefully wrought narrative of the stages that brought him to the moment of saying "I believe."

Lewis was a notably popular and prolific writer with a remarkably diverse literary output that included, besides the spiritual autobiography, children's books, scholarly works, science fiction, volumes on Christian doctrine, and an intensely personal description of his grief-ridden quarrel with God after his wife's death. And more to the point, he was perhaps the finest Christian apologist writing in English in the twentieth century.

His books have been adapted for stage, screen, and television, and he has been the subject of several biographies as well as a film based on his life. Although there is no telling just how many people he has reached, the number is certainly well up in the millions. But his emergence as a Christian writer was long in coming. In *Surprised by*

Joy, the autobiographical story of his religious conversion, he provides a careful, mostly candid explanation of how he passed, in his words, "from Atheism to Christianity". And he adds, "How far the story matters to anyone but myself depends on the degree to which others have experienced what I call 'joy.' "[1]

Clive Staples Lewis was born on November 29, 1898, in Belfast, Northern Ireland, the second of two sons of well-to-do parents with bookish tastes and a weak attachment to Anglicanism. As a child, he had three experiences of intense desire for something—what, he could not tell—that he calls "joy", and these experiences remained embedded in his memory. Only in the experience of conversion to Christ many years later did he begin to understand those experiences to have been "a pointer to something other and outer".[2] But with his mother's death from cancer in 1905, "all settled happiness, all that was tranquil and reliable", vanished from his life.[3]

Three years later, his father sent him to a boarding school in England, a "vile" place where he adopted High Church Anglicanism as his religion. This was followed by a second boarding school that impressed Lewis favorably and where, "with the greatest relief", he stopped being a Christian. His reasons for doing that included a bout of scrupulosity, early interest in the occult, loss of belief in the antiquity of Christianity, and, at the age of fourteen, a "successful assault of sexual temptation". Under the influence of a favorite teacher, he now became "a converted Pagan living among apostate Puritans".[4]

---

[1] C. S. Lewis, *Surprised by Joy: The Shape of My Early Life* (New York: Harcourt, Brace and World, 1955), vii.
[2] Ibid., 238.
[3] Ibid., 21.
[4] Ibid., 69.

At this time, he also acquired a taste for the music of Richard Wagner and for the Nordic myths that provide the storylines for several Wagnerian operas. "Sometimes I can almost think that I was sent back to the false gods ... to acquire some capacity for worship against the day when the true God should recall me to himself", he writes.[5]

The next stop was an English public school where the emphasis on achieving and retaining high social status disgusted Lewis. Needless to say, he remained an atheist, although one plagued by contradictions: on the one hand, he held that God did not exist, while on the other hand, he was angry with God for not existing. To prepare him for Oxford, his father sent him next to a retired headmaster, William T. Kirkpatrick, who proved to be an excellent though idiosyncratic tutor as well as an atheist, whom Lewis describes as "a 'Rationalist' of the old, high and dry nineteenth-century type".[6] Without any overt effort, Kirkpatrick casually supplied the boy with fresh grounds for his lack of faith.

Having become an atheist and a materialist with a reviving interest in magic and the occult, Lewis now did what he considered one of his worst deeds: allowing himself to receive confirmation and First Communion despite his disbelief with the sole intent of thus avoiding having to discuss his religious situation with his father. This, in fact, was typical of his relationship with a parent who undoubtedly wished to be a good father to his two sons but who was simply too absorbed in his own ideas and prejudices to be capable of any real empathy with them.

World War I was in its second year in 1916, when Lewis entered Oxford with his sights already set on the army.

---

[5] Ibid., 77.
[6] Ibid., 170.

After completing an officer training course, he found himself, on his nineteenth birthday, arriving in the trenches in France as a second lieutenant. During an assault the following April, he was seriously wounded by a British shell that fell short of its intended target. Of the rest of his wartime experience he has little to say.

A brilliant postwar academic career at Oxford followed, and during this time, as always, Lewis read widely. Among the authors who impressed him were the Scottish fantasy writer George MacDonald; essayist and novelist G. K. Chesterton, not yet a Catholic but on his way to becoming one (he converted in 1922); and French philosopher Henri Bergson, whose writings persuaded him to abandon materialism in favor of idealism and led Lewis to believe, if not precisely in God, then at least in "the Absolute". Reflecting on this period of his life, Lewis issues a tongue-in-cheek warning: "A young man who wishes to remain a sound Atheist cannot be too careful of his reading." For now he made the disconcerting discovery that his favorite authors, past and present, were all religious while all the nonbelievers were "thin".[7]

While teaching at Oxford, Lewis became one of the Inklings, an informal group of literary men who met for conversation and the reading of one another's books. Along the way, too, Lewis read Chesterton's *The Everlasting Man* and found in it a persuasive Christian interpretation of history, which moved him, along with thinking Chesterton "the most sensible man alive", to conclude that Christianity itself was also "very sensible". But he was even more moved by the testimony of the unnamed "hardest boiled of all the atheists I ever knew", who, while paying a visit, unintentionally rattled Lewis by remarking

[7] Ibid., 191.

that "the evidence for the historicity of the Gospels was really surprisingly good" and adding, "It almost looks as if it had really happened once."[8]

Similar testimony was provided by J.R.R. Tolkien, future author of the immensely popular *Lord of the Rings* trilogy, Oxford professor, and a Catholic, along with other friends. Their testimony led Lewis in time to see for himself that the gospel was radically different from any pagan myth and "no person was like the Person it depicted ... not a god, but God."[9]

In an interview years later with the Christian Broadcasting Network, Lewis remarked that he had come to see that his own decision played a comparatively small part in his conversion: "I was the object rather than the subject in this affair.... What I heard was God saying, 'Put down your gun and we'll talk.'" Taking an honest look at himself, however, he did not like what he saw: "a zoo of lusts, a bedlam of ambitions, a nursery of fears, a harem of fondled hatreds. My name was legion." He continued fretting for some time. And then "in the Trinity Term [spring] of 1929 I gave in and admitted that God was God, and knelt and prayed: perhaps, that night, the most dejected and reluctant convert in all England.... The hardness of God is kinder than the softness of men, and His compulsion is our liberation."[10]

But one final step remained to be taken—the definitive turning point: acceptance of the Incarnation, of Jesus Christ as Son of God in the full sense that Christian faith gives that name. One sunny morning in 1931, Lewis and his brother, Warren, decided to visit Whipsnade Zoo, a

[8] Ibid., 235.
[9] Ibid., 236.
[10] Ibid., 229.

popular six-hundred-acre zoo and safari park in Derby-shire. Lewis tells what happened: "When we set out I did not believe that Jesus Christ is the Son of God, and when we reached the zoo I did. Yet I had not exactly spent the journey in thought. Nor in great emotion.... It was more like when a man, after long sleep, still lying motionless in bed, becomes aware that he is now awake."[11]

Lewis became, and remained, a conservative Anglican with generally traditional theological views. After teaching at Oxford for twenty-nine years, in 1954 he became first holder of the chair of medieval and Renaissance litera-ture at Cambridge University. Two years later, he married Joy Davidman, an American woman who had divorced her abusive husband. After her death from cancer in 1960, Lewis wrote a book called *A Grief Observed*, in which he recorded his painful struggle to accept God's will.

Besides scholarly works, his books include a very pop-ular series of children's stories set in an imaginary land called Narnia; three science fiction novels; *The Screwtape Letters*, an analysis of the psychology of temptation cast in the form of letters from a senior devil to his nephew; and *Mere Christianity*, probably the best known of his sev-eral works of popular theology and apologetics. Begun as a series of BBC radio talks during the wartime years of 1942 to 1944, the book seeks to present Christianity in a fresh light appropriate to that particular time and place: "Chris-tianity agrees with Dualism that this universe is at war", he writes. "But it does not think this is a war between independent powers. It thinks it is a civil war, a rebellion, and that we are living in a part of the universe occupied by the rebel. Enemy-occupied territory—that is what this world is. Christianity is the story of how the rightful king

[11] Ibid., 237.

has landed, you might say landed in disguise, and is calling us all to take part in a great campaign of sabotage."[12]

C. S. Lewis died of kidney failure on November 22, 1963, the same day that President John F. Kennedy was assassinated. In 2013, he was honored with a place in Poets' Corner in Westminster Abbey. His spot is marked by a Lewis quotation: "I believe in Christianity as I believe that the Sun has risen, not only because I see it, but because by it I see everything else."[13]

Lewis clearly underwent conversion. But what are we saying when we say that of him or, for that matter, of anyone else? There are several possible meanings, and they are by no means mutually exclusive.

The words "convert" and "conversion" are commonly used of someone who moves from adherence to one religion or belief system to another and of that movement, that quasi-local shift in allegiance and personal identity. So we say, "Fred converted from being a Baptist to being a Methodist" or "Beth converted from the Presbyterian church to the Episcopal church." Of Lewis, we might say that he converted from atheism to Christianity.

Although this is a legitimate way of speaking, conversion also has another, rather different sense. In fact, the *Catechism of the Catholic Church* speaks of a "first" and a "second" conversion, neither of which necessarily involves changing religious affiliation. Baptism, the *Catechism* explains, is the place for the "first and fundamental" conversion, which

---

[12] C. S. Lewis, *Mere Christianity* (New York: HarperCollins, 1952), 45–46.
[13] C. S. Lewis, "Is Theology Poetry?" (lecture, Oxford Socratic Club, November 6, 1944).

brings "the forgiveness of all sins and the gift of new life"; while the second conversion is a matter of somehow changing the orientation of the whole of one's prior way of life— "the movement of a 'contrite heart,' drawn and moved by grace to respond to the merciful love of God who loved us first".[14] Using this terminology, we can say of C. S. Lewis that he worked at living out this second conversion from 1931 until his death three decades later.

Here Dietrich von Hildebrand's account of those who "hunger for justice" and, as such, might be described as wholly converted is helpful: "Their passion for the victory of the good constitutes a virtual menace to the framework of ordinary people's lives.... What they seek is not merely whatever is naturally valuable and *as such* glorifies God: it is (beyond that) the supernatural life, the victory of the God-Man Christ, the salvation of souls, the growth of the Mystical Body of Christ, and man's transformation in Christ.... The empire of Christ over our souls, as well as in all other souls, must become the paramount theme of our lives."[15] The use of military terminology is reminiscent of Lewis, while the rest recalls Lewis' words on his Poets' Corner marker, likening his belief in Christianity to his belief in the rising of the sun, "not only because I see it, but because by it I see everything else".

Over the centuries, others have grasped what that means; whether they lived it out successfully in their own lives is another matter. Writing of the painter Caravaggio, who is said to have lived a distinctly disordered life, and of his masterful painting *The Calling of Saint Matthew* in the Church of Saint Louis of France in Rome, the art historian

---

[14] *CCC* 1427, 1428, quoting Ps 51:17; cf. Jn 6:44; 12:32; 1 Jn 4:10.

[15] Dietrich von Hildebrand, *Transformation in Christ* (San Francisco: Ignatius Press, 2001), 306–7.

Elizabeth Lev remarks that the painting makes conversion "look like love at first sight, the first fear of change immediately replaced with the compelling light of truth".[16]

Poet and essayist Kathleen Norris, speaking of *Mere Christianity*, says the vision of faith presented there by Lewis is "not a philosophy or even a theology" but "a way of life ... what Christ asked of us in taking on our humanity, sanctifying our flesh, and asking us in turn to reveal God to one another".[17] And Lewis clearly speaks from his own experience of conversion in its radical sense when, at the end of that book, he writes,

> It is no good trying to "be myself" without Him. The more I resist Him and try to live on my own, the more I become dominated by my own heredity and upbringing and surroundings and natural desires.... I am not, in my natural state, nearly so much of a person as I like to believe: most of what I call "me" can be very easily explained. It is when I turn to Christ, when I give myself up to His Personality, that I first begin to have a real personality of my own....
>
> Until you have given up your self to Him you will not have a real self....
>
> But there must be a real giving up of the self. You must throw it away "blindly" so to speak. Christ will indeed give you a real personality: but you must not go to Him for the sake of that. As long as your own personality is what you are bothering about you are not going to Him at all.... Keep back nothing. Nothing that you have not given away will be really yours. Nothing in you that has not died will ever be raised from the dead. Look for yourself, and you will find in the long run only hatred, loneliness, despair, rage, ruin,

---

[16] Elizabeth Lev, "Love at First Sight: A Baroque Master's Vision of Conversion", *Catholic Exchange*, September 21, 2023, https://catholicexchange.com /love-at-first-sight-a-baroque-masters-vision-of-conversion/.

[17] Kathleen Norris, introduction to *Mere Christianity*, xix.

and decay. But look for Christ and you will find Him, and with Him everything else thrown in.[18]

Lewis' eloquence might lead one to imagine that he is talking about only those special individuals whom we call "the saints". But Lewis would not have agreed. Rather, I believe his view was the same as that expressed in the *Catechism*: "Nevertheless the new life received in Christian initiation has not abolished the frailty and weakness of human nature, nor the inclination to sin that tradition calls *concupiscence*, which remains in the baptized such that with the help of the grace of Christ they may prove themselves in the struggle of Christian life."[19] "This is the struggle of *conversion* directed toward holiness and eternal life to which the Lord never ceases to call us."[20]

At the very end of *Surprised by Joy*, Lewis rather surprisingly tells the reader that by this point in the story he is telling, he had largely lost interest in the subject of "joy" with which he had begun.

[18] Lewis, *Mere Christianity*, 225–27.
[19] *CCC* 1426, cf. Council of Trent (1546): DS 1515.
[20] *CCC* 1426, cf. Council of Trent (1547): DS 1545; *LG* 40.

Caryll Houselander

(September 29, 1901–October 12, 1954)

Her Own Suffering Taught Her How to Heal

In giving the biography of her friend Caryll Houselander the subtitle *Divine Eccentric*, Maisie Ward clearly
knew what she was doing. Divinity was up to God, of
course, but there was no question that Houselander was
eccentric. Besides that, as Ward, her publisher, was well
aware, she was also one of the finest spiritual writers of
modern times.

Along with possessing a rare gift with words, Houselander had a remarkable talent for empathy with suffering
people. Partly it reflected the fact that she knew what it
was to *see* the suffering Christ in others (more about that
below). And partly, her gift for healing the mental and
emotional pain of others arose from her own not incon-
siderable experience of suffering.

Make no mistake, though: by no stretch of the imagination was Houselander a plaster saint. She smoked
heavily (eventually she quit, but only after long delay), enjoyed gin and wine, and had a sharp tongue frequently
employed at the expense of people who annoyed her—a
fault she often indulged and no less often repented. But
here, as in much else, she found a solution in Jesus. The
secret of fulfillment, atonement, and joy, she wrote, lies in
being given, as she had been, "the life of Christ—Christ's

mind to adore with, Christ's love to love with, Christ's sacrifice to atone with".[1]

Caryll Houselander was born on September 29, 1901, in Bath, England, the second of two daughters of religiously nonpracticing parents. When she was six, her mother had her and her sister baptized as Catholics before entering the Church herself. Houselander accordingly called her autobiography *A Rocking-Horse Catholic*, in contrast with "cradle" Catholics who are Catholic from infancy.

Her early childhood was unremarkable, but when she was nine, her parents separated, an event that delivered a lifelong shock to their children, to whom the abrupt breakup of their family came without warning. Many years later, Caryll was to write of herself, "I am a frightened, abject creature ... because in youth I was broken right across (psychologically!), early and irrevocably, so started pretty well defeated."[2] Following her separation from Caryll's father, her mother sent Caryll away to a convent school. The girl was relatively happy during her five years there, and it was there that she had the first of three life-changing visions.

Although most of the nuns were French, one was Bavarian, isolated by her language and—these being the early days of World War I, with French-German animosities running high—by her nationality. One day, Houselander came upon the woman polishing shoes by herself and weeping as she did. The child stood there, not knowing what to say or do, and Houselander writes, "At last, with an effort, I raised my head, and then—I saw—the nun was crowned with the crown of thorns. . . . I said to her, '*I* would not cry, if I was wearing the crown of thorns

[1] Quoted in Maisie Ward, *Caryll Houselander: Divine Eccentric* (Providence, R.I.: Cluny Media, 2021), 256.

[2] Ibid., 223.

like you are.'... I sat down beside her, and together we polished the shoes."[3]

After a long stretch of ill-health—one of many she was to suffer—the fifteen-year-old girl, self-described as being by then "a confirmed prig and morbidly shy", was sent by her mother to an English convent school.[4] Here she found herself bewildered and alienated by her wealthy schoolmates' heartiness and enthusiasm for sports. Not surprisingly, she made no friends. And here, too, her generally negative view of things began to extend to the Church.

Now her mother, living in London by then, brought Caryll there to help her run a boardinghouse to support herself and her daughters. It was there, one evening in July 1918, on her way to buy potatoes for dinner, that she had her second great vision, a particularly spectacular one. Filling the sky she saw a gigantic Russian icon of Christ the King crucified. She did not know it at the time, but a few hours earlier, Russia's Czar Nicholas II, together with his family, had been executed by Bolshevik revolutionaries. A day or two later, she saw the murdered czar's face for the first time in a newspaper photograph. And it was the face of Christ the King whom she had seen in her vision.

Time passed. Houselander attended art school and left the Catholic Church. She looked into other Christian churches as well as Judaism and Buddhism, but none suited her. Meanwhile, she eked out a living at odd jobs and pursued a bohemian lifestyle that included falling in love with a professional spy named Sidney Reilly (said to be the model for Ian Fleming's fictional James Bond), who broke her heart by marrying another woman and eventually was apprehended and executed by the Bolshevik secret police.

[3] Caryll Houselander, *A Rocking-Horse Catholic: A Brief Exercise in Autobiography* (New York: Sheed and Ward, 1955; Providence, R.I.: Cluny Media, 2024), 78–79. Citations refer to the Cluny edition.
[4] Ibid., 91.

One day in Hyde Park, she stopped to listen to a young speaker for the Catholic Evidence Guild. The man was Frank Sheed—author and Catholic apologist. He and his wife, Maisie Ward, were later to be Houselander's publishers and friends. Almost despite herself, she was impressed by what she heard that day in the park. "It was the Catholic Church", she says, "but it was the Church being Christ, not waiting for the people to come in, but coming out to the people. It was *really*, in a way that I could not understand, Christ following His lost sheep—of whom I was one."[5]

Not long after came Houselander's turning point—her third vision. She explains,

> I was in an underground train, a crowded train in which all sorts of people jostled together, sitting and strap-hanging—workers of every description going home at the end of the day. Quite suddenly I saw with my mind, but as vividly as a wonderful picture, Christ in them all. But I saw more than that; not only was Christ in every one of them, living in them, dying in them, rejoicing in them, sorrowing in them—but because He was in them, and because they were here, the whole world was here too, here in this underground train; not only the world as it was at that moment, not only all the people in all the countries of the world, but all those people who had lived in the past, and all those yet to come.
>
> I came out into the street and walked for a long time in the crowds. It was the same here, on every side, in every passer-by, everywhere—Christ.[6]

The vision lasted a few days, then gradually faded, but it had permanent consequences that from then on shaped Houselander's life.

[5] Ibid., 144–45.
[6] Ibid., 150–51.

Now she returned to the Church, supporting herself modestly by wood-carving commissions and articles she wrote for Catholic magazines. Along with her visions, she also had a natural gift—which she took quite matter-of-factly—for extrasensory perception: she not uncommonly "saw" things that had not happened yet or were happening at a distance without any ordinary way for her to know of them. She also reported "seeing" angels and saints—such as Saint Jude walking down a street in London and, she reported, "dressed in something like a seaman's jersey".[7]

In the World War II years, she served as a volunteer first-aid nurse and fire warden during the bombing of London and as a government censor. The war also brought the publication of her first book, *This War Is the Passion*, which, based on her faith in the Mystical Body of Christ, is a meditation grounded in the idea that the war was a shared participation in Christ's sufferings. Appearing in the United States in 1941 and in Great Britain the following year during the war's darkest hours, the book established her as a writer with something important to say. Other books, many of them still in print today, followed in a steady stream from the Sheed and Ward publishing house.

"The originality of Caryll's work", writes Maisie Ward, "came partly from its complete reality. Spiritual books are so often written in cliches by people remote from life. Caryll was living in the midst of human suffering at its intensest—she was aware of it all the time ... and I think we see from her correspondence that her own sufferings had taught her the art of healing."[8]

As Caryll's reputation spread, troubled people or their caregivers more and more sought her out by letter or in person. This "unending siege of callers" weighed heavily

---

[7] Ward, *Caryll Houselander*, 133.
[8] Ibid., 170–71.

on her time and physical strength, but her sense of duty moved her to respond, and her correspondence documents the extraordinary effort she devoted to responding.[9]

Ward's biography contains many of her responses, such as this:

> Prayer *should* be a deep inner rest, something which calms you and increases your *trust* (the more it *does* increase your trust, the more it gives you inner peace and rest).
>
> In a busy and harassed life, this *could* not be the result of prayer, if the most important thing were how many words you can get said in a day! Lots of deeply holy and prayerful people *can't* say *one*, even at Mass. Prayer, as the Catechism tells us, is "raising the heart and mind to God"—there need be no words, but only an inexpressible adherence to God, an attitude of mind and heart, a simple wordless desire to be one with Him. This makes it inevitable that one recognizes His Will for one at the moment in every circumstance, and knows that every act, however trivial, done in this spirit, is done for His glory and *is* prayer.[10]

Caryll Houselander died of cancer at the age of fifty-three in 1954. Her last words, spoken to a close friend who had been watching at her bedside, were "You must be very tired."[11]

Houselander was not a theologian, but she read widely in religious literature, and her own lived experience provided vivid instruction concerning much that she read. Her flowering as a spiritual writer largely coincided with the upsurge

[9] Ibid., 192.
[10] Ibid., 240.
[11] Ibid., 300.

of interest in the understanding of the Church as the Mystical Body of Christ following the publication in 1943 of Pope Pius XII's encyclical *Mystici Corporis Christi*. But the doctrine had its origins much earlier, in the writings of Saint Paul, who employs it in several of his letters. For example, in Romans 12:4–5 he writes, "As in one body we have many members, and all the members do not have the same function, so we, though many, are one body in Christ." Pope Pius expresses the same idea: "As in nature a body is not formed by any haphazard grouping of members but must be constituted of organs, that is of members, that have not the same function and are arranged in due order; so for this reason above all the Church is called a body."[12]

Within the fundamental unity of the body's members, both sources point out, there is a necessary diversity of function. Saint Paul: "Having gifts that differ according to the grace given to us, let us use them: if prophecy, in proportion to our faith; if service, in our serving; he who teaches, in his teaching; he who exhorts, in his exhortation; he who contributes, in liberality; he who gives aid, with zeal; he who does acts of mercy, with cheerfulness" (Rom 12:6–8). And Pope Pius: "[The Church is called a body in that she] is constituted by the coalescence of structurally united parts, and that she has a variety of members reciprocally dependent."[13]

Saint Paul and Pope Pius also both emphasize that Christ's presence in the Church is individual as well as corporate: he is present in each member of the Church, as Paul says of himself: "It is no longer I who live, but Christ who lives in me" (Gal 2:20). Pope Pius also speaks of this indwelling realized in and through the Spirit of Christ:

[12] Pius XII, encyclical letter *Mystici Corporis Christi* (June 29, 1943), no. 16.
[13] Ibid.

"Christ our Lord ... permeates His whole Body and nour-
ishes and sustains individual members according to the
place they occupy in the body.... It is He who, through
His heavenly grace, is the principle of every supernatural
act in all parts of the body."[14]

Caryll Houselander was particularly drawn to the idea
of Christ's presence in individual persons, derived especially from the third of her three great visions in which she
"saw" Christ in the other riders on a London subway and,
for several days following, in everyone else she encountered. Near the end of *A Rocking-Horse Catholic*, she did
her best to explain what this meant to her. Recalling that,
up to then, she had been troubled about "the Blessed Sacrament's being put into the hands of sinners", she wrote,
"I saw that it is the will of Christ's love *to* be put into the
hands of sinners, to trust Himself to men, that He may
be *their* gift to one another, that *they* may comfort Him
in each other, give Him to each other. In this sense the
ordinary life itself becomes sacramental, and every action
of anyone at all has an eternal meaning."[15]

Maisie Ward declares the volume titled simply *Guilt* to
be Houselander's "richest" book. First published in 1951,
three years before her death, it is an extended reflection on
the phenomenon that Houselander calls "ego-neurosis"
and is drawn largely from the author's interactions in person and by correspondence with people suffering from this
affliction. At the conclusion, she writes,

We do not see Christ in man, but now we *know* that he
is in man, in those of our own household in whom he is
most hidden from us. A continual seeking for him in them,

[14] Ibid., no. 55, 57.
[15] Houselander, *A Rocking-Horse Catholic*, 152.

an unfailing effort to penetrate his disguise and to dis-
cover in which of the infinite variety of ways possible to
him Christ is living in each one of those who are part of
our own lives, cannot fail to draw off the concentration
from self; and the necessity to serve Christ in others cannot fail to break down the barriers of self-protection, self-
consciousness and self-love which lead to the frustration of
the uncured ego-neurotic.[16]

And ultimately, she concludes, it all comes together
for the afflicted individual in the Eucharist: "Finally he
receives Christ into his soul again, and in communion
with him becomes one with all men, and goes out from
Mass to carry Christ into the world in which he lives his
daily life. This is the concentrated plan of man's life, end-
ing as life itself will end when it is lived on this plan, with
'Deo gratias—Thanks be to God.'"[17]

[16] Caryll Houselander, *Guilt* (New York: Sheed and Ward, 1951), 277.
[17] Ibid., 279.

Saint Josemaría Escrivá

(January 9, 1902–June 26, 1975)

"Nothing but God's Grace and Good Humor"

When speaking of the origins of Opus Dei, Saint Josemaría Escrivá, its founder, made no extravagant claims for himself. He often explained that he was at the time only a twenty-six-year-old priest with nothing but good humor and—most important—God's grace. True as that was, though, it was indeed he who suddenly "saw" Opus Dei one day in 1928 and realized that God had assigned him the task of shepherding this new entity.

Today Opus Dei—the Work of God—is a vigorous worldwide organization with more than ninety-six thousand members. Although often described as conservative, Opus Dei has pioneered the idea that laypeople are called to achieve sanctity and that, rather than withdrawing from the world, the laity should seek sainthood in secular settings—job, family life, recreation, and all the rest. The founder and the Work, as members call it, thus anticipated the Second Vatican Council, which took the unprecedented step of declaring in its Constitution on the Church that the "universal call to holiness" extends to the laity as much as to priests and nuns: "All the faithful of Christ of whatever rank or status, are called to the fullness of the Christian life and to the perfection of charity."[1]

At the start, nonetheless, there was nothing to suggest the role Josemaría Escrivá would play in God's plan and certainly no reason to suppose it would involve a significant new vision of laypeople and their place in the Church.

His origins were unremarkable. He was born on January 2, 1902, in Barbastro, a small town in northern Spain, the second of six children of José and Dolores Escrivá. Three of his younger sisters died at an early age, and when he was two years old, Josemaría himself contracted a virulent infection and was not expected to live. His parents promised to make a pilgrimage to a Marian shrine if he recovered. He did, and the pilgrimage was made.

In 1914, the textile firm where his father was a partner went bankrupt. José Escrivá made it a point of honor to pay off creditors from his own resources, and the family, until then moderately well-to-do, was reduced to near poverty. Soon they moved to another town, Logroño, where they could live more cheaply and where the elder Escrivá worked as a clerk in a clothing store until his death in 1924. Monsignor Escrivá later declared his "holy pride" in his father, saying, "I believe he has a very high place in heaven, because he managed to bear in such a dignified, marvelous, Christian way all the humiliation that came with finding himself out on the street."[2]

By then, the young man was a seminary student preparing for the priesthood. He had been moved to take this step partly by the sight of footsteps made in newly fallen

[1] Vatican Council II, Dogmatic Constitution on the Church *Lumen Gentium* (November 21, 1964), no. 40.

[2] Quoted in Andrés Vázquez de Prada, *The Founder of Opus Dei: The Life of St. Josemaría Escrivá*, vol. 1, *The Early Years* (Princeton, N.J.: Scepter Publishers, 2001), 43–44.

snow by a Discalced Carmelite—a visible expression of self-sacrifice for love of God that moved him deeply—and partly by a growing sense that God had something particular in mind for him that would require him to be a priest. "I had hints that our Lord wanted something, but many years passed before I found out what it was", he later wrote. "In the meantime I thought of the blind man in the Gospel, because I was blind with regard to my future and the service that God wanted from me. Like him, I kept repeating, *Domine, ut videam! Domine, ut sint!* [Lord, that I may see! Lord, let it be!]. I repeated this for years: 'Let it be. May this thing that you want come about.... Give light to my soul.'"[3] The light did not come, but prayer was clearly the path to it.

After attending the seminary in Logroño, Josemaría continued his studies at the San Carlo Seminary in Zaragoza. There he also began studying civil law at the local university in the belief that he would need income from professional work—probably as a teacher—in order to support his mother, his older sister, and his younger brother. He was ordained a priest for the Diocese of Zaragoza in March 1925 and offered his first Mass for his father. For two years, he did parish work; then, with his bishop's permission, he moved in April 1927 to Madrid, intending to continue legal studies at Central University.

Having found a position as chaplain of the Foundation for the Sick, a charitable program conducted by a group called the Apostolic Ladies of the Sacred Heart of Jesus, the young priest busied himself bringing the sacraments to the poor in the city's slums. Equipped daily with lists of people to visit, his biographer writes, he found himself regularly riding the streetcar or else "sloshing through

---

[3] Ibid., 129.

mud in the winter, trekking through dust clouds in the summer, stepping in manure and tromping through piles of garbage" to carry out his ministry.[4] And all the time, he continued praying to be enlightened regarding the mysterious something God wanted of him. "Fac, ut sit!" (Do it, let it be!), he prayed.

On the morning of Tuesday, October 2, 1928, the day set aside by the Church to honor the guardian angels, he was making a retreat with five other priests at the Vincentian Fathers' headquarters. Alone in his room, he was reviewing his notes on the hints he had been receiving for years when something unexpected happened. Although he kept details to himself, especially those of a personal nature, in later years he described the heart of it like this: "I received an illumination *about the entire Work* while I was reading those papers. Deeply moved, I knelt down— I was alone in my room, at a time between one talk and the next—and gave thanks to our Lord, and I remember with a heart full of emotion the ringing of the bells of the Church of Our Lady of the Angels."

Fearful at first, he became conscious of the words "Do not be afraid!"

In the Old Testament and in the New, God and celestial beings spoke them to raise people out of their misery and dispose them for a dialogue of illumination and love, and for a confidence about things that are seemingly impossible.... *Ne timeas* ["Do not be afraid"] communicates to them an indestructible security, sparks in them impulses of faithfulness and dedication, gives them clear ideas about how to fulfill his most lovable will, and inflames them to hasten toward goals beyond merely human reach.[5]

[4] Ibid., 213.
[5] Ibid., 220–21.

Clear and forceful as this communication was, many important matters remained unspecified. At first, for instance, the youthful founder believed only men could be members of this new group, and it took another illumination, on February 14, 1930, to show him it was intended for women too. As for a name, it had none at the start, and in the end, it was another priest, not Escrivá, who suggested calling it Opus Dei.

In the early years, too, growth was slow. Only gradually did Escrivá begin to attract members and young professionals to the Work, and expansion was halted entirely in 1936 by the outbreak of the Spanish Civil War. Realizing that his life was in danger in Madrid from anticlerical leftist militias, Escrivá hid for months—first in a mental institution, then in the Honduran consulate—before he and several members of the Work made their way north, including an arduous journey through the Pyrenees to Andorra and, reentering Spain, finally to Burgos, where he spent the rest of the war ministering to young men serving in the Nationalist army.

The civil war was barely over before World War II broke out, further delaying Opus Dei's international expansion. But in 1946, the founder transferred headquarters to Rome, and the Work began to spread rapidly in Europe and beyond—North America, Latin America, Africa, Asia, and the Far East. It began in the United States in the winter of 1949.

By this point, the story of Monsignor Escrivá's life had, practically speaking, become the story of Opus Dei's growth. But the Work's purpose remained as it had been from the beginning. In a homily preached on October 8, 1967, to members at the University of Navarra—an institution Escrivá had founded in Pamplona, Spain—he deplored the depiction of the Christian way of life as "something exclusively spiritual—or better, spiritualistic—something reserved for pure, extraordinary people who remain aloof from the contemptible things of this world". When people adopt this attitude, he warned, "churches become the setting par excellence of the Christian way of life. And being a Christian means going to church, taking part in sacred ceremonies, getting into an ecclesiastical mentality, in a special kind of world, considered the antechamber to heaven, while the ordinary world follows its own separate course. We flatly reject this deformed vision of Christianity."[6]

Alongside their secularity, however, members of Opus Dei follow a clear, specific program intended to nurture a solid interior life. "A personalized, fully thought-out plan will enable us to accomplish more with the time we have available, and will help us realistically to set our goals", Monsignor Escrivá wrote.[7] The plan includes spiritual direction, daily Mass and Communion, weekly confession, daily mental prayer and recitation of the Rosary, participation in a yearly retreat and monthly days of recollection, regular reading of the New Testament and other spiritual reading, and some form of apostolic activity.

In canonical terms, Opus Dei is a personal prelature, a new form of institutional structure created by the Second Vatican Council to serve the pastoral needs of particular groups of persons.[8] In 1982, Pope Saint John Paul II made Opus Dei the first, and so far the only, personal prelature.

---

[6] Josemaría Escrivá, "Passionately Loving the World", 2004, The Studium Foundation, https://www.stjosemaria.org/pltw/pdf/Passionately-Loving-the -World-full-text.pdf.

[7] Josemaría Escrivá, *A Plan of Life* (Strongsville, Ohio: Scepter Publishers, 2019), 1.

[8] Vatican Council II, Decree on the Ministry and Life of Priests *Presbyterorum Ordinis* (December 7, 1965), no. 10.

By far, the most numerous members are laypeople, most of them married and with children, who, along with their membership in the Work, remain attached to their own dioceses. A small group, the "numeraries", are celibate and live with other numeraries in Opus Dei centers. "Associates" follow a similar plan of life but live alone or with their families. "Numerary assistants" have the special apostolate of maintaining the upkeep of the organization's centers. Slightly more than two thousand priest numeraries belong to the prelature, and two thousand diocesan priests are members of the Priestly Society of the Holy Cross and receive spiritual support and encouragement from it while remaining incardinated in their own dioceses and subject to their diocesan bishops.

While keeping its institutional presence to a minimum to avoid becoming bogged down in institutions, Opus Dei does have some. These include international centers in Rome for the formation of men and women numeraries, universities in several countries, secondary schools, and some other training facilities. It began activities in the United States in Chicago in 1949 and now has around three thousand U.S. members. There are Opus Dei centers in Boston, Chicago, Dallas–Fort Worth, Houston, Los Angeles, Miami, Milwaukee, New York, Pittsburgh, Princeton, San Antonio, San Francisco, South Bend, Saint Louis, Urbana-Champaign, and Washington, D.C. It has eight conference centers for retreats and seminars in the United States and eight secondary schools. Its U.S. headquarters is in New York.

Members do not wear any special insignia or otherwise seek to advertise their membership, lest they appear to be setting themselves apart as a special group. But neither do they conceal that they are members; their centers are publicly known as such, and nonmembers are welcome to participate in Opus Dei retreats and in days (or mornings or evenings) of recollection. Most students in schools conducted by the Work are not members.

Books by Monsignor Escrivá and others are available for sale from a publishing house called Scepter Publishers. Far and away his best-known title is *The Way*, a volume for use in personal meditation and prayer containing 999 aphorisms and anecdotes, many of the latter drawn from the author's pastoral experiences. It begins this way: "Don't let your life be sterile. Be useful. Blaze a trail. Shine forth with the light of your faith and of your love."[9] First published in 1939, *The Way* has been translated into forty-three languages with a total printing of more than 4.5 million copies. Two other small volumes drawn from the same sources—*The Forge* and *Furrow*—have also been published, as have collections of the founder's homilies.

In 2022, following a reorganization of the Roman Curia, Pope Francis directed that Opus Dei will no longer report to the curial dicastery for bishops but to the dicastery for priests. He specified that, in keeping with its founding charism, the prelate should not be a bishop, as Monsignor Escrivá's first two successors had been. The current prelate, Monsignor Fernando Ocáriz, welcomed the changes as "an opportunity to go more deeply into the spirit that our Lord instilled in our Founder".[10]

And what was that spirit? The answer may lie in something Saint Josemaría said about the virtue of humility: "It's not a lack of humility to be aware of your soul's progress. That way you can thank God for it. But don't forget that you are a beggar, wearing a good suit ... on loan."[11]

[9] Josemaría Escrivá, *The Way* (New York: Scepter Publishers, 1954), 1.

[10] "Letter from the Prelate regarding the Motu Proprio 'Ad charisma tuendum'", Opus Dei, July 22, 2022, https://opusdei.org/en/article/letter-from-the-prelate-regarding-the-motu-proprio-ad-charisma-tuendum/.

[11] Escrivá, *The Way*, 608.

A few weeks before his death, he visited the men in formation in the Work's Cavabianca formation center outside Rome and spoke to them in these affectionate, somewhat teasing terms:

> You have so much road that's already been traveled, you can't go wrong. With what we have done in the theological realm—a new theology, my children, and the good kind—and in the realm of canon law; with all that we've done with the grace of the Lord and his Mother, with the providence of our father and lord Saint Joseph, with the help of the guardian angels, you can't go wrong now, unless you are scoundrels. Let us give thanks to God. You already know that I am not needed here, that I've never been needed.[12]

On June 26, 1975, after paying a morning visit to a center of women members in Castel Gandolfo, where he felt dizzy and had to lie down, he returned to Rome and there died of cardiac arrest. He was canonized in 2002 by Saint John Paul II, who considered him "among the great witnesses of Christianity".[13] Seventy-four years before, the young priest who had nothing but "God's grace and good humor" would probably have been astonished at hearing that.

While Saint Josemaría Escrivá broke new ground in speaking of the spirituality of the laity, he was not the first to develop that subject. As early as the seventeenth century, Saint Francis de Sales argued that, quite as much as priests

[12] Andrés Vázquez de Prada, *The Founder of Opus Dei: The Life of St. Josemaría Escrivá*, vol. 3, *The Divine Ways on Earth* (Princeton, N.J.: Scepter Publishers, 2005), 547.

[13] Antonio Gaspari, "A New Way for the Church?", *Inside the Vatican*, June/July 1995, accessed on EWTN, https://www.ewtn.com/catholicism/library/new-way-for-the-church-9847.

and religious, laypeople were also called to lead holy lives. In his *Introduction to the Devout Life*, de Sales provided a well-developed outline for laypeople attempting to do that. And in the closing years of the nineteenth century, Saint Thérèse of Lisieux directed her Little Way to laypeople (as well as to the clergy and religious) as a trusty method for using the little things of ordinary life as stepping stones to sanctity.

There are clear echoes of Thérèse's "spiritual childhood" in the chapters of Escrivá's book *The Way* called "Spiritual Childhood" and "Life of Childhood". And he writes, "Spiritual childhood demands submission of the mind, which is harder than submission of the will. In order to subject our mind we need not only God's grace, but a continual exercise of our will as well, denying the intellect over and over again, just as it says 'no' to the flesh. And so we have the paradox that whoever wants to follow this 'little way' in order to become a child, needs to add strength and manliness to his will."[14]

His emphasis on the importance of personal vocation similarly converges with insights others have had. Thus, one finds this idea in Saint Paul's doctrine of the Church as the Mystical Body of Christ. One finds it in many places in Vatican II. And one finds it in Pope Saint John Paul II, especially in his first encyclical, *Redemptor Hominis*, in which he writes that each Christian, "in imitation of Christ's example [has] the duty to demand of himself exactly what we have been called to, what we have personally obliged ourselves to by God's grace, in order to respond to our vocation".[15]

The spirituality promoted by Saint Josemaría is noteworthy, too, for assigning a central place to everyday

[14] Escrivá, *The Way*, 856.
[15] John Paul II, encyclical letter *Redemptor Hominis* (March 4, 1979), no. 21.

work—including not only jobs but also tasks such as house-
work and schoolwork. Not only is work a context and
occasion for spiritually meritorious activity, he insists, but
work itself is sanctified by one who works with the intention of making it a means to growing in holiness. "Without
work", he writes, "we will not sanctify ourselves. The reason for this is that work is the material we have to sanctify
and the instrument of our sanctification." And he adds,

> We must love every type of human work, because work
> is our means for the sanctification of souls and for the
> glory of God. And if work, any honest human work, is
> the means, no one will be able to place any shores on this
> immense sea of apostolate....
>
> In this way our work becomes supernatural, because
> its end is God, and we do our work with him in mind as
> an act of obedience. We must not leave that place where
> the Lord's call has taken us by surprise. We must, instead,
> turn our whole life into God's service: our work and our
> rest, our tears and our smiles. In the fields, in the work-
> shop, in the study, in public life: we must remain faithful
> to our habitual way of earning our living and turn every-
> thing into an instrument for sanctification and an apostolic
> example.... It is not enough to work a lot; rather, we
> must work with supernatural outlook, because otherwise
> we will not receive blessings from heaven.[16]

Vatican II echoes this in its Constitution on the Church
Lumen Gentium when, having proclaimed the universal call
to holiness, it says of "those who engage in labor" that in
"their daily work they should climb to the heights of holiness and apostolic activity".[17]

[16] St. Josemaría Escrivá, *The Collected Letters*, vol. 1 (Strongsville, Ohio: Scepter Publishers, 2021), 142–45.

[17] *Lumen Gentium*, no. 41.

Afterword

Saint Teresa of Avila

(March 28, 1515–October 4, 1582)

Some readers may find it a mite odd to speak about Saint Teresa of Avila in winding up a book about turning points of people who made a definitive commitment to God's will for them. It is not that Teresa did not accept God's will. Certainly she did. But she also was one of the greatest of mystics, and her life of mystical experience was so extraordinary that she can hardly be said to have understood enough about it at the start to commit herself to it then, while the fact that eventually she wrote about it as well as anyone has ever done is really beside the point.

But hold on. For Saint Teresa's turning point was perhaps not what you suppose. To begin with, it came before Saint Teresa abandoned prayer.

"What's that?" the skeptical reader says. "How could it happen that this great saint and future Doctor of the Church ever gave up praying?"

Well, actually, she did not give up praying entirely. Instead, as an obedient young Carmelite nun, Teresa obeyed the rule of her order and continued to practice community prayer alongside her sisters in religion. But she did give up prayer of another kind—mental prayer. And she dropped the practice for what seemed to her at the time a very good reason: humility. After accusing herself of indulging in a variety of "vanities", here is how she explains it in her autobiography:

> The devil, beneath the guise of humility, now led me into the greatest of all possible errors. Seeing that I was so utterly lost, I began to be afraid to pray. It seemed to me better, since in my wickedness I was one of the worst people alive, to live like everyone else; to recite, vocally, the prayers that I was bound to say; and not to practice mental prayer or hold so much converse with God, since I deserved to be with the devils, and, by presenting an outward appearance of goodness, was only deceiving others.[1]

She continued her boycott of mental prayer for a year or more, believing all the while that she was doing the right thing and thereby growing in humility. But then she had the good fortune to take as her confessor a wise Dominican, Father Vicente Barron, who told her to receive Communion regularly and, learning of her prayer boycott, instructed her to resume praying, since, as she says, it "could not possibly do me anything but good".

For Saint Teresa of Avila, this was her turning point. Not that everything went smoothly for her thereafter. On the contrary, she suffered many trials, along with ill-health, but she also persevered in prayer, for, as she puts it, "by that time it was no longer in my power to give up prayer, because He who desired me for His own in order to show me greater favors held me Himself in His hand."[2]

There is a lesson in Saint Teresa's turning point, one that applies to us all. The key to progress in the spiritual life lies in having a plan of life organized around the Eucharist,

---

[1] *The Life of Teresa of Jesus*, trans. E. Allison Peers (Garden City, N.Y.: Doubleday Image Books, 1960), 96.

[2] Ibid., 105.

the regular practice of mental prayer, and a few other pious practices and involving consultation with a sensible, orthodox spiritual director. It is unlikely the result will be a continuing series of profound mystical experiences, but having adhered to it consistently over time, we shall find that this is how we, too, have placed ourselves in God's hand.

> I spent nearly twenty years on that stormy sea, often falling in this way and each time rising again, but to little purpose, as I would only fall once more.... Nevertheless, I can see how great was the Lord's mercy to me, since He gave me courage to practice prayer. I say courage, because although we are always in the presence of God, it seems to me that those who practice prayer are specially so, because they can see all the time that He is looking at them....
>
> There is no place here for fear, but only desire. Even if a person fails to make progress or to strive after perfection, he will gradually gain a knowledge of the road to heaven. And if he perseveres, I hope in the mercy of God, whom no one has ever taken for a friend without being rewarded.[3]

And that, I trust, explains why, if given the chance, I would nominate Saint Teresa of Avila as Patroness of Turning Points.

---

[3] Ibid., 110.